Love of Jesus

Love of Jesus

The Heart of Christianity

RICHARD E. CREEL

RESOURCE *Publications* · Eugene, Oregon

LOVE OF JESUS
The Heart of Christianity

Copyright © 2010 Richard E. Creel. All rights reserved. Except for brief quotations in critical publications or reviews, no part of this book may be reproduced in any manner without prior written permission from the publisher. Write: Permissions, Wipf and Stock Publishers, 199 W. 8th Ave., Suite 3, Eugene, OR 97401.

Resource Publications
An Imprint of Wipf and Stock Publishers
199 W. 8th Ave., Suite 3
Eugene, OR 97401

www.wipfandstock.com

ISBN 13: 978-1-60899-322-2

All quotations from the Bible come from *The Oxford Annotated Bible*, edited by Herbert G. May and Bruce M. Metzger. New York: Oxford University Press, 1962. And *The New Oxford Annotated Bible*, 3rd edition, edited by Michael D. Coogan. Oxford, UK: Oxford University Press, 2001.

Manufactured in the U.S.A.

Love of Jesus is dedicated to him who inspired it
and to all those who love and serve him.

Contents

Preface   ix

Introduction   xi

PART I   WHY ADMIRE AND LOVE JESUS?

1   Reasons to admire Jesus   3

physically tough • mentally tough • highly intelligent • mentally quick • independent • courageous • hated hypocrisy • emphasized justice, mercy, and humility • condemned but forgave sin • not a charlatan • warned against doomsday prophets • did not abuse his power • emphasized well-being over rules • was wise • encouraged use of reason

2   Reasons to love Jesus   49

respect for women • love of children • voluntary suffering for others • happiness • humor • friendship • reality and immortality of the individual • the great physician • dignity of the individual • critical of prejudice • humility • generosity • mothers and fathers • loyalty • emotions • temptation • hope • stress and peace • work • mercy • sympathy • good news • priorities • love • God with us

PART II LOVERS OF JESUS

   3 What makes a person a Christian? 99

   4 Denominations and Love of Jesus 103

   5 Reasons to doubt Jesus? 110

      Predestination • Ask and it will be given • Divorce • Tolerating evil and extending charity • Hate your parents •. Insensitivity to animals • The world did not end • Dangerous recommendations • But they did die

   6 Jesus accepted doubters 122

      Conclusion 127

Preface

IF YOU WOULD LIKE to read a thoughtful, earnest treatment of many reasons for admiring and loving Jesus, then this is a book for you! If you admire and love Jesus but have difficulty identifying yourself as a Christian because of intellectual difficulties with this or that aspect of Christianity, then this is a book for you, too! In *Love of Jesus* I am reaching out to lay people and to pastors. I will not be engaging in scholarly debate about the historical Jesus—debate such as thinkers like Marcus Borg, John Crossan, Timothy Johnson, and John Spong engage in. Their research and debates are fascinating and important, but I have a different agenda. I want to take at face value the New Testament stories about Jesus and ask of them why we should admire and love the man who inspired them. And then I want to ask how we should follow him and relate to one another as Christians. Those are the things that this book is about.

I once told a dear friend that it seemed like my entire adult life had been spent trying to become a Christian. Writing this book has been like the final stage of that long birthing process. The labor has been filled with stress and anguish at times, but it has finished with a sense of joy—not only for having completed it, for having "given birth"—but more so for the peace and solidity that I now feel with Christ and the Church. Imperfect as my newborn child is—and as any book about Jesus must be—I find deep satisfaction in it, and I hope that you, too, will find it to be of value.

Introduction

THIS BOOK HAS TWO aims. Its first aim is to say why Jesus of Nazareth is worthy of our admiration, love, and devotion. People who already believe this do not need to be convinced, of course, but they, too, I believe, will be enriched and encouraged by what I present in the following pages. People who are not already convinced, but whose minds and hearts are changed by what I say, will want to know how to go about being devoted to this Jesus who is so worthy of our devotion. To address that need is my second aim; it involves a discussion of what it means to be a Christian and of denominations. The two parts of this book correspond to these two aims.

In part 1, chapter 1, I provide many stories and quotations from the Bible to show why Jesus is worthy of our *admiration*. In part 1, chapter 2, I provide many examples and quotations from the Bible to show why Jesus is worthy of our *love*. In part 2 I build on part 1 to set forth what I think is at the heart of being a Christian, namely, love of Jesus. For readers who already belong to a church, I will explain (1) how this way of understanding what it means to be a Christian might lead to a new understanding of one's own denomination and (2) how different denominations are related to one another. For readers who do not belong to a church, this new understanding of what it means to be a Christian might lead to a new understanding of oneself, and it could lead to joining an existing denomination as a full member or an affiliate, or it could lead to establishment of a new denomination. In all of these cases I believe our lives will be enriched and elevated by intelligent devotion to Jesus.

In my first two chapters you may sometimes think that a reason I give for *admiring* Jesus should have been in the chapter of reasons for *loving* Jesus, or that a reason I give for loving Jesus should have been in the chapter of reasons for admiring Jesus. As long as you conclude that a reason I give is a good reason for admiring Jesus or loving him—but that I have put it in the wrong chapter—I am satisfied. You may sometimes also think that a reason I give is a good reason for both admiring *and* loving Jesus and therefore should be cited in both chapters of part 1. I would probably agree, but to minimize repetition I have limited most reasons to one chapter or the other.

Finally, sometimes you may think that a reason I give is not persuasive. I would be surprised (but elated!) if you *do* think that all of my reasons are "home runs." Nonetheless, I will be satisfied in the end if you agree that there are enough reasons in this book to justify admiring and loving Jesus. As we explore these reasons, please keep in mind that (1) I am not listing them in order of importance, (2) the length of what I write about a reason is not an indication of how important it is, and (3) there are even more reasons than these for admiring and loving Jesus.

Now, a personal note. When I read a book that contains statements of opinion and interpretation I find it tiresome for the author to keep saying "I think" and "I believe" and "It is my opinion that," so I'm not going to do that very often. Yet I am concerned that if I do not do that, then you, dear reader, may think I am dogmatic or close-minded. So please think of this whole book as bracketed by the statement: "The following is what I, Richard Creel, think at this time." If you think differently, please tell me so, and perhaps I, too, will think differently at a future time—thanks to you.

Part I

Why Admire and Love Jesus?

1

Reasons to Admire Jesus

IN THIS CHAPTER I will present reasons to admire Jesus. Among such reasons are these: Jesus was (1) physically tough, (2) mentally tough, (3) highly intelligent, (4) mentally quick, (5) independent, (6) and courageous, plus he (7) hated hypocrisy, (8) emphasized justice, mercy, and humility, (9) forgave but condemned sin; (10) was not a charlatan; (11) warned against doomsday prophets, (12) did not abuse his power; (13) emphasized well-being over rules; (14) was wise, and (15) encouraged us to use our minds in religious matters. These fifteen traits are not exhaustive and are not listed in order of importance, but they should be sufficient to establish that Jesus is worthy of profound admiration by anyone and everyone.

In order to illustrate and elaborate the traits above, I will make many references to the New Testament, and especially the Gospels, which are our main sources of information about Jesus' life and teachings. There are four Gospels, each written by a different disciple of Jesus. If you are not familiar with the authors of the Gospels, please keep in mind that when I refer to Matthew, Mark, Luke, or John, I am referring either to the Gospel which has that name or to the author of that Gospel. Also, when I refer to a specific location in a Gospel, I will usually do so by citing the abbreviated name of the author, the chapter, and the verses, in that order. For example, (Mt 1:1) means "The Gospel According to Matthew, chapter 1, verse 1". (Mk 2:2–4) means "The Gospel According to Mark, chapter 2, verses 2 through 4." Likewise for the Gospel According to Luke (Lk) and the Gospel According to John (Jn).

I also want to alert you that in this chapter I will not be focusing on stories about miracles performed by Jesus. There are many reports in the New Testament of miracles that Jesus performed. I will touch on some of them, but because I am writing for skeptics and searchers as well as believers, I am not going to emphasize miracles in this chapter. What I want to emphasize is that there are many reasons to admire Jesus apart from the miracles that were attributed to him. Indeed, there are many reasons to admire Jesus even if you have difficulty believing in miracles or don't believe in them at all.

One final qualification is this: I realize we can admire someone without loving her or him. Indeed, sometimes we should not love someone whom we admire. In that case the person usually has one characteristic we admire and another characteristic we abhor. For example, we might admire Hitler's brilliance as an orator while being repulsed by his willfully ignorant, hate-filled personality. Of course we can also love someone without admiring her or him. Sometimes we love a friend or relative who has succumbed to drugs but do not admire him or her. With Jesus, however, there are many reasons to both admire and love him, so now let's look into fifteen reasons for admiring him.

1. JESUS WAS PHYSICALLY TOUGH

Jesus was a physically tough person. His father was a carpenter, so given the fact that in Jesus' time, sons usually took up the same kind of work as their fathers, it should be no surprise that Jesus was a carpenter for 20 years or more. (In Matthew someone says of Jesus, "Is not this the carpenter's son?" (Mt 13:54–55) And in Mark someone says, "Is not this the carpenter, the son of Mary?" (Mk 6:3)

As a carpenter until he was about 30 years old, Jesus must have been strong of body (Lk 3:23). I've split, cut, and carried plenty of firewood, so I know that wood is heavy stuff! And Jesus would have carried a lot more wood than I have. He would have acquired further strength from using the tools of a carpenter, such as axes and hatchets, planes and saws, hammers and drills.

As a boy I had a friend whose father was a carpenter. One day the father invited me to saw some wood. I think he probably invited me with an inner smile, knowing what I was in for (I had never sawn wood before). Sawing looks so easy: the saw isn't very heavy, and you just draw the blade back and forth over the top of the wood. And it was easy for the first 30 seconds. But I was amazed at how quickly my muscles tired and started to ache from a little sawing until soon my muscles seized up and I couldn't even move my arm! So I'm sure that Jesus' muscles were well-developed. Carpentry also leads to inevitable cuts, bruises, splinters, and busted fingernails. I don't think there can be any doubt that Jesus' hands were strong, calloused, and probably scarred.

Finally, consider that Palestine, where Jesus lived, was a very hot country. There were no air-conditioners or even electric fans back then, so for most of the year carpentry was hot, sweaty, exhausting work. We can admire the fact that as a carpenter Jesus was a strong, skilled person in a valuable, physically demanding occupation.

Consider also that Jesus was no "couch potato." In addition to the skills, strength, and toughness that he developed as a carpenter, he walked miles and miles on the hot, dusty, rocky roads of Palestine. Moreover, he climbed hills and mountains in order to get away, think and pray.

At the end of his life Jesus was arrested, imprisoned, beaten, spat on, and had a crown of thorns mashed onto his head. After being deprived of a night of sleep, and surely also of food and water, and after being beaten brutally and losing blood, he carried a considerable distance the cross on which he was to be crucified, until he finally collapsed from fatigue. Those were afflictions that Jesus could have chosen to avoid, but he did not. He was tough enough to take them on and endure them. In street talk, he was "tough as nails."

But what about his closest followers? Were they, or at least most of them, physically tough? The answer is definitely "yes." Some of Jesus' followers were what today might be called "real men." Peter, Andrew, James, and John were fishermen. Fishing for a living was hard, dangerous work then as it is now. Those men were strong, rugged, and courageous. In one story Peter says that he and Andrew had been fishing all night—not with a rod and reel or machine-operated equipment but with a large, heavy net that they had to put out and pull in by hand. The story says they had no luck that night. They were tired and discouraged, yet when Jesus showed up at dawn and asked them to cast out their net one more time, they did. These strong, tough men admired Jesus enough to accept him as their leader when he called them—even when they were very tired (Mk 1:16–20; Jn 21:1–8).

Consider also the physical condition of two unnamed disciples who, after the death of Jesus, were walking from Jerusalem to Emmaus, a distance of about seven miles. According to Luke, the resurrected Jesus joined them along the way. The disciples did not recognize him at first, so the three of them went along, walking and talking. The disciples were completely captivated by the personality of this stranger and what he had to say, so they invited him to share their evening meal in Emmaus and stay overnight. During the meal Jesus, as he had done at "the last supper" with his disciples, took bread and blessed it; then the disciples realized who their guest was. Jesus soon vanished, we are told, and those disciples were so excited that they *immediately* walked *back* to Jerusalem to tell the other disciples! On the dusty, rocky, hilly roads of Israel, that was an impressive physical accomplishment. At a fast pace, that round trip of 14 miles would have taken 3 hours of walking or more (about 1.5 hours each way).

Perhaps some of Jesus' followers were couch potatoes, but, as we have seen, some of his closest followers were not (see Lk 24:13–35). Moreover, as nearly everyone knows, Peter—the aforementioned fisherman, the foremost of Jesus' apostles, and the leader of the early church—was a blustery, aggressive guy. When Caiaphas, the high priest of the Jews, sent a large crowd with swords and clubs to arrest Jesus in the Garden of Gethsemane, Peter had a sword, drew it, and cut off the ear of one of the men whom Caiphas had sent to arrest Jesus. Peter was ready to do battle—but Jesus told him to cool it (Mt 26:47-54; Jn 18:1-11).

James and John were similarly inclined to aggressive action. They were nicknamed "The Sons of Thunder," and we can see why from the following story. When a Samaritan village refused to extend hospitality to Jesus, James and John said to him, "Lord, do you want us to command fire to come down from heaven and consume them?" Jesus said "no" and rebuked them, but their feisty personalities are evident from that story (Lk 9:51-56).

I think it is interesting and important to realize that most of the apostles (the men who worked most closely with Jesus) were not wealthy hedonists or angry insurrectionists or members of an isolated monastic group. They were typical members of the Jewish working class in their time. They knew and accepted the responsibilities of family and community life; they knew the dangers, fatigue, and tedium of a life of physical labor.

Lest I leave the impression that Jesus' apostles came only from the laboring class, it should be noted that the apostle Matthew was not a fisherman or a carpenter but a tax collector. Indeed, another reason for admiring Jesus is that he was admired and followed by people from so many different categories: men and women, elderly and children, laborers and professionals. Outside the circle of Jesus' twelve apostles, but among his followers, were respected, wealthy men of the community. For example, Zaccheus was a chief tax collector (Lk 19:1-10). Joseph of Arimathea was "a respected member of the council" and "a rich man." Indeed, Joseph of Arimathea had enough wealth and influence that after Jesus was crucified, Joseph went to the Roman administrator Pilate, and convinced Pilate to give Jesus' body to him (Mt 27:57–58); then Joseph buried Jesus in a new tomb that Joseph owned and in which he had planned to be buried himself. Only the wealthy could afford a tomb of their own; obviously, Joseph had wealth, respect, and influence. Another well-to-do admirer of Jesus was Nicodemus, who was a Pharisee and "a leader of the Jews." Nicodemus helped Joseph of Arimathea prepare Jesus' body to be placed in Joseph's tomb (Jn 3:1–2; 19:38–42).

2. JESUS WAS MENTALLY TOUGH

In addition to being physically tough, Jesus was mentally tough. By that I mean he was strong of will and highly self-disciplined. As we might say today, it was impossible to knock him off target or distract him from his mission. Because of his conception of his mission in life, and his belief in God's support for it, he was tempted to do things to prove that he had the power that he believed he had, and he was tempted to take personal advantage of that power. For example, when he retreated into the desert after he was baptized by his cousin John the Baptist, Jesus fasted for many days—which in itself takes great strength of will. When he gradually became very hungry, we are told that Satan challenged him by saying (I paraphrase), "*If* you are the Son of God, prove it! You are hungry, you are the Son of God, so turn these stones to bread and feed yourself!" Jesus was famished, so understandably he was tempted to use his power to turn a stone into a loaf of bread that would end his terrible hunger.

When he refused to yield to that temptation (which must have taken tremendous strength of will), Satan took a different tack and said, "*If* you are the Son of God, you can leap off the pinnacle of the Temple in Jerusalem and not be harmed. God will protect you. So jump! *Prove* that you are the Son of God!" But Jesus refused to challenge God in that way. (Notice how clever Satan was: first he tried to get Jesus to challenge God to turn stones into bread and thereby drive a wedge between himself and God; when that didn't work, Satan tried to get Jesus to kill himself by jumping off the Temple!)

Next Satan said (again I paraphrase), "Okay. You aren't going to prove you are the Son of God, so you don't know whether you are or not. But *I* know that all the kingdoms and glory of the world have been given by God to *me*, so if you fall down and worship me, if you become *my* son, the Son of Satan, I will give all the wealth and glory of the world to *you*!" So if Jesus fell down and worshipped Satan, he would have not only bread but anything his heart desired! But Jesus knew that Satan was *a creature* who existed by the will of God and who ruled, if at all, over a very small portion of reality. Satan was not *the Creator* who ruled over *all* of reality. So Jesus stayed focused mentally and resisted these enormous physical, emotional, and spiritual temptations.

Nor was he later deflected from his mission when his family members thought he was deranged and tried to talk him out of his mission; nor was he deflected by the fact that his disciples tried to dissuade him from going to Jerusalem and facing arrest, or by the fact that some people laughed at him, scorned him, and said he was working for Satan (which was an ironic claim after the heroic way in which Jesus had stood up to Satan's temptations in the desert!). Moreover, Pharisees, Sadducees, scribes, and chief priests tried repeatedly to trip up Jesus or get him to prove, on their terms, that he was indeed from God. But he stayed on course in spite of all.

In summary, it took enormous mental toughness for Jesus to stick to his mission in the face of so many hostile, derisive people—and even people who loved him but doubted his judgment. He withstood enormous physical suffering, family resistance, and social hostility in order to do what he believed in. He fasted in a harsh desert environment. While suffering on the cross for hours under a sweltering sun, severely dehydrated from sweating and bleeding, he refused to accept a tainted drink of liquid to slake his thirst. When we consider that Jesus could have avoided all or most of this abuse and suffering by never launching out on his ministry or by abandoning it along the way (as many people would have been happy for him to do), then we realize that the man was more than admirably strong in mind and spirit—he was awesome.

3. JESUS WAS HIGHLY INTELLIGENT

Jesus was not only tough; he was intelligent. When he was 12 years old his parents took him to Jerusalem, where the most highly respected scholars of Judaism lived. During this time, Jesus went to the Temple—the center of Jewish worship and scholarship—and engaged in discussion with the great teachers of Israel. We are told that he not only listened, but also asked questions. Those teachers, we are told, "were amazed at his understanding and answers" (Lk 2:47).

Some eighteen years later, when Jesus began his public ministry at about age 30, we learn that he could read. We know this because we are told that he went to a synagogue in Nazareth, stood, and read the Scriptures aloud. Then he commented on them, and, according to St. Luke, "all spoke well of him, and wondered at his gracious words which proceeded out of his mouth" (Lk 4:22). Some of those present asked, "Where did this man get this wisdom?" "Is not this the carpenter's son?" (Mt 13:54–55) "Is not this Joseph's son?" (Lk 4:22) The Gospel of Mark quotes someone who asked, "Is not this the carpenter, the son of Mary?" (Mk 6:3)

Obviously, carpenters were not expected to read, speak eloquently, and comment wisely on Scripture. After all, carpenters were not educated in that society. Yet Jesus could read and his teachings were impressive. On one occasion, according to St. John, "About the middle of the feast [of Tabernacles] Jesus went up into the temple and began to teach. The Jews were astonished at it, saying, 'How does this man have such learning, when he has never been taught?'" (Jn 7:14–15) In addition, a study of Jesus' teachings in the Gospels shows that he was brilliant with metaphors, analogies, and stories. See, for example, his story about seeds that fall on various kinds of soil (Mk 4:13–20). In brief, anyone who admires intelligence should admire Jesus.

4. JESUS WAS MENTALLY QUICK

Some people are very intelligent but not mentally quick. For example, they do not think quickly of perceptive replies to what others say. Jesus was quick of mind, sharp and insightful, as well as intelligent. After he began his public ministry, members of various groups tried to trap him by posing puzzles or questions that were intended to get him into trouble no matter what he said in reply. But Jesus could tell when people were trying to trap him with questions, and he dodged their traps in clever ways.

For example, St. Matthew tells us that after the chief priests and elders tried to trip up Jesus but failed, "Then the Pharisees went and took counsel how to entangle him in his taLk And they sent their disciples to him, along with the Herodians, saying, 'Teacher, we know that you are true, and teach the way of God truthfully, and care for no man; for you do not regard the position of men. Tell us, then, what you think. Is it lawful to pay taxes to Caesar, or not?'" That was a dangerous question for Jesus to answer. If he said, "No, it is not lawful to pay taxes to Caesar," then the Pharisees would have reported him to the Roman authorities and he would have been arrested for opposing the Roman government. If he had said, "Yes, it is lawful to pay taxes to the Roman government," then the Pharisees would have portrayed him to Jews as a traitor to Israel, which was being oppressed and exploited by the Romans.

So what did Jesus do? Matthew says that Jesus, aware of the malice of those Pharisees, said to them, "'Show me the money for the tax.' So they brought a coin to him. Jesus then asked, 'Whose likeness and inscription is this [on the coin]?' They said, 'Caesar's.' Then he said to them, 'Render therefore to Caesar the things that are Caesar's, and to God the things that are God's.'" Matthew reports that when the Pharisees heard that, "they marveled, and they left him and went away" (Mt 22:15–46). Jesus' reply was stunningly astute. Not only did he escape the murderous intentions of those Pharisees, he proposed two profound questions for all of us to think about: What do we owe to God, and what do we owe to the government?

Sometimes Jesus turned the table on his questioners by replying with questions that *they* could not answer—or dared not answer. For example, when the scribes accused him of casting out demons by the power of the prince of demons (which was his accusers' way of saying that Jesus was in league with the devil), he turned the logic of his accusers against them by replying as follows: You agree that casting out demons is good, and you concede that I am casting out demons, so either I am doing good by the power of Satan or by the power of God. If I am doing good by the power of Satan, then Satan is divided against himself and will fall, and that is good, so you should be happy to leave me alone and allow me to continue undermining the power of Satan. If, however, I am undermining Satan by the power of God, then that, too, is good, and, again, you should be happy to allow me to continue on my way. Either way, you should be pleased. So what's the problem? They had no answer (Mk 3:22–27).

5. JESUS WAS INDEPENDENT

We admire people who "have a mind of their own"—which means something like having a keen sense of what one wants to do and having the will and discipline to do it, even if other people disagree with what you want to do or even if they want you to do it in a different way. Jesus was definitely independent minded. Many people admired and followed him, but he was not dependent on their approval or their ideas of what *they* wanted him to do.

As we saw earlier, even at age 12 his independence showed through. It was then that his parents took him to Jerusalem to celebrate Passover at the Temple, as they did every year. This time, however, after Jesus' parents left Jerusalem to return home, he stayed behind in the Temple to listen to and talk with the master teachers of Israel. His parents were part of a caravan of families and friends from Galilee who had gone together to Jerusalem, no doubt including aunts, uncles, and cousins of Jesus, plus friends of the family, so after Passover all these folks traveled back toward Galilee for a day before Jesus' parents realized he was not with any of his aunts, uncles, cousins, or friends in the caravan.

Mary and Joseph, deeply worried, had to backtrack to Jerusalem looking for Jesus. St. John tells us, "After three days they found him in the temple, sitting among the teachers, listening to them and asking questions." "When his parents saw him they were astonished; and his mother said to him 'Child, why have you treated us like this? Look, your father and I have been searching for you in great anxiety.'" Jesus replied, "Why were you searching for me? Did you not know that I must be in my Father's house?" Even at twelve Jesus had a sense of mission from which he could not be deflected (Lk 2:41–52).

The preceding is one of those stories about which we would like to know more. It sounds like Jesus was inconsiderate toward his parents, but there may have been a good explanation. For example, perhaps Jesus had told them that he wanted to stay behind and talk with the rabbis, but his parents thought he was kidding (after all, that was a pretty wild thing for a working-class kid to want to do or think he could do!). In any case, John reports that

Jesus then returned to Nazareth with his parents "and was obedient to them" (Jn 2:41–51). And we must not forget that at that time Jesus was age 12 and was therefore within a whisker of being considered by the Jewish community to be a grown man, at age 13.

Once Jesus began his public ministry, around age 30, he continued to be independent. For example, early one morning he left a crowd of people and went out to a lonely place to pray. His disciples found him and said, "Everyone is searching for you." I'm sure he knew that, but he had other priorities. He needed to pray in solitude, so he quietly went off by himself. When he came back the people said they wanted him to stay there with them, but he told them he had to go to other towns as well as theirs, and again he left them. On another occasion when his mother and brothers came in search of him, to divert him from his mission, he made it clear that his family was now not his blood relatives but the people who supported his mission (Mk 3:31–35).

Of course some people did not support Jesus' mission and even laughed at him, but that didn't deter him either (Mt 13:23–25). And when an enthusiastic crowd tried to make him king, Jesus withdrew from them and went into the hills by himself because he knew he could not fulfill his mission through political power and status. "My kingdom," he said, "is not from this world" (Jn 6:14–15; 18:36). Hence, he was consistently and admirably independent—not allowing others to alter his mission or divert him from it.

6. JESUS WAS COURAGEOUS

Jesus was courageous. In Gerasa there was a naked, deranged man who lived among the tombs of a cemetary. People tried more than once to confine him with chains, but he was so strong that he wrenched them apart and broke them to pieces. Moreover, he was always crying out and bruising himself with stones. What a frightening, miserable figure he must have been. But Jesus did not run when he landed on the shore of Gerasa and this madman approached him. Jesus stood his ground, and it was the demoniac who was frightened. Then the man was cured by Jesus and "clothed in his right mind." What a terrifying, touching segment of a movie that story would make. And when Jesus began to leave, the formerly fierce man begged to go with him! What an enormous testimony to Jesus' courage and goodness (Mk 5:1–20). (See also the story of the Gadarene demoniacs in Mt 8:28–34. Matthew says that the Gadarene demoniacs were "so fierce that no one could pass that way." But Jesus did pass that way, and he rid the demoniacs of their demons.)

Jesus' courage was also exhibited in the fact that he touched lepers. In the ancient world, people were understandably terrified of lepers because of fear that leprosy was contagious. According to Leviticus 13–14, a person diagnosed to be leprous "shall wear torn clothes and let the hair of his head be disheveled; and he shall cover his upper lip and cry out, 'Unclean, unclean'" as he walks along the streets. And as long as he is diagnosed to be leprous, "He shall live alone; his dwelling shall be outside the camp." Conversely, non-leprous people were not supposed to even come close to lepers, and if they did, they became "unclean" and had to follow elaborate procedures in order to be cleansed and accepted back into the community.

In light of the preceding information, consider the courage that Jesus exhibited in the following situation, as reported by St. Matthew. "When Jesus had come down from the mountain [after delivering what is called "the Sermon on the Mount," Mt 5–7], great crowds followed him; and there was a leper who came to him and knelt before him saying, 'Lord, if you choose, you can make me clean!' [Jesus] stretched out his hand and touched him, saying, 'I do choose. Be made clean!'" "Immediately," we are told, "his leprosy was cleansed" (Mt 8:1–4). Again, in view of the extreme fear of leprosy that was cultivated in Jews from childhood on, and in view of strong religious sanctions against contact with lepers, Jesus showed breathtaking courage (and compassion) by reaching out and touching the pitiable leper who begged him for help.

Yet the most impressive expression of Jesus' courage is this: he knew that if he continued on his mission he would end up dying a terrible death by crucifixion, the typical punishment that Roman authorities inflicted on Jewish troublemakers. Nonetheless, he did not at any of numerous opportunities abandon his mission and walk away from his followers, nor did he plead for mercy from Pontius Pilate or Herod Antipas, the Roman rulers who held his fate in their hands.

7. JESUS HATED HYPOCRISY

Jesus hated hypocrisy. See, for example, the entire 23rd chapter of Matthew. Hypocrisy usually consists of claiming to be, or presenting oneself to be, better than one is.

Because it consists of trying to deceive people into thinking one is something one is not, hypocrisy is a form of lying. Jesus was especially disturbed by religious hypocrisy, that is, by people who presented themselves as being religious when they were not. Jesus aimed his harshest words at hypocrites who preached one thing but did another, who pretended to be merciful but placed heavy burdens on people, who devoured widows' houses yet pretended to be generous, who strutted about publicly and loved to be served by others and called by flattering names but who did not follow the will of God and tried to prevent others from doing so. They talked the talk, but they didn't walk the waLk In brief, while claiming to live according to God's injunction that we "act justly, love mercy, and walk humbly," they did quite the opposite. (See Micah 6:8, to which we will return in the next section.)

Jesus told his disciples to refuse to be called by honorific names. "He who is greatest among you," he told his followers, "shall be your servant; whoever exalts himself will be humbled, and whoever humbles himself will be exalted" (Mt 23:1–13). Hypocrites, he said, are like whitewashed tombs—they look nice on the outside but are foul and rotten on the inside (Mt 23:27–28; also Lk 11:37–40). Using another analogy, Jesus pointed out that religious hypocrites are people who claim to be religious but do not bear the fruits of religion. (John the Baptist said this earlier, Mt 3:7–10; Jesus continued this message in Mt 7:15–20).

Hitting close to where we all live, Jesus criticized people for the hypocrisy of criticizing others when they should be focusing on their own faults. In his humorous way Jesus said that a person who avoids self-criticism but loves to criticize other people is like someone who ignores a log sticking out of his own eye in order to point out to someone else that he has a speck in his eye. (Wouldn't that make a great cartoon? Mt 7:5–23)

Jesus also pointed out the hypocrisy of people who made a public show of how religious they were. In particular, he criticized people who made sure the public knew what they were giving to the Temple so they would be praised, and he criticized those who "love to stand and pray in the synagogues and at the street corners, so that they may be seen by others," and those who "disfigure their faces so as to show others that they are fasting." By contrast, Jesus thought that our gifts and our prayers and our fasting should be kept between us and God (Mt 6:1; 23:2).

Along the same line, Jesus pointed out the hypocrisy of wealthy people who made a big show of tithing money to the temple in order to make it appear that they were religious when what they gave they could easily afford. By contrast, Jesus pointed out, poor people who gave money they could barely afford were more admirable (Mk 12:38–44). To make matters worse, sometimes the money of the wealthy had been acquired by acts that were unjust or unmerciful. Sure, Jesus said, we should support the temple, but without neglecting "the weightier matters of the law: justice and mercy and faith" (Mt 23:23–24). To do otherwise is hypocrisy. To avoid hypocrisy, Jesus believed, we must follow the wisdom of the prophet Micah, who said of God, "He has told you, O mortal, what is good; and what does the Lord require of you but to do justice, and to love kindness, and to walk humbly with your God?" (Micah 6:8)

Jesus also illustrated the nature of hypocrisy by telling a story about two sons. One morning their father asked them to go work in his vineyard Working in the vineyard was hot, hard work. One son said he would go. The other son said he would not go. However, the son who said he would go did not go, whereas the son who said he would not go changed his mind and did go. The first son pretended to be a good son, but he wasn't. The other son wasn't perfect either. He initially told his father he would not go, but then he changed his mind and did go. Jesus asked his disciples, "Which of the two did the will of his father?" All agreed it was the second son. The second son was temporarily rebellious, but the first son was hypocritical (Mt 21:28–32).

Rather than a story that Jesus *told*, here is a story about Jesus himself—a story in which hypocrisy rears its ugly head again. Jesus, we are told, cured a woman who for eighteen years had been unable to stand up straight. However, he cured her in a synagogue on a Sabbath in spite of the fact that Jews were forbidden to "work" on the Sabbath. The leader of the synagogue criticized Jesus in front of the people in the synagogue, saying there were six days during the week for Jesus to cure people, so he ought not to have cured the woman on a Sabbath. Curing people is work, the synagogue leader said, and we are not suppose to work on the Sabbath. Jesus replied, "You hypocrites! Does not each of you on the Sabbath untie his ox or his donkey from the manger, and lead it away to give it water? And ought not this woman, a daughter of Abraham whom Satan bound for eighteen long years, be set free from this bondage on the Sabbath day?" (Lk 13:10–17)

On another occasion on which Jesus was criticized for curing someone on the Sabbath, he pointed out to his critics that if they had a sheep that fell into a ditch on the Sabbath, they would get it out right away. They wouldn't wait until the next day—and getting a sheep out of a ditch was certainly work! Hence, it was hypocritical of those folks to criticize Jesus for working on the Sabbath by helping a human in distress (Mt 12:1–14). If Jesus' critics had said, "We're not saying, 'Don't cure these people.' We're saying, 'Wait until after the Sabbath to do it,'" I think he would have replied, "I will not be here then. I must move on, so I must cure them now or not at all. Would you have me leave this woman with her affliction simply because it is the Sabbath?" To claim to love mercy, as Scripture enjoins us to do, yet to leave an afflicted person uncured because it is the Sabbath—the day above all on which we should do the will of God—would be hypocritical. And so we see, once again, that Jesus' condemnation of hypocrisy was unremitting.

8. JESUS EMPHASIZED JUSTICE, MERCY, AND HUMILITY

What does it mean to be religious? The prophet Micah, as we have seen, answered that question in a piercing, haunting way when he said, "What does the Lord require of you but to do justice, to love kindness, and to walk humbly with your God?" (Micah 6.8) Jesus agreed, and consequently, as we just saw in the section on hypocrisy, he was disturbed by people who were not just or kind or humble but presented themselves as such,. To Jesus, true religion meant following Micah 6:8, and it meant loving

God with all of your heart, mind, soul, and strength, and your neighbor as yourself (Mk 12:28–31).

Here is a collage of statements from Jesus' Sermon on the Mount (Mt 5–7) which show how deeply concerned he was with the humility of which Micah spoke: "Beware of practicing your piety before men in order to be seen by them." "When you give alms, sound no trumpet before you, as the hypocrites do in the synagogues and in the streets, that they may be praised by men." "When you pray, you must not be like the hypocrites; for they love to stand and pray in the synagogues and at the street corners, that they may be seen by men." "And when you fast, do not look dismal, like the hypocrites, for they disfigure their faces that their fasting may be seen by men" (Mt 6:1–18). Because criticizing others can be hypocritical, Jesus said: Don't worry about the speck in someone else's eye; worry about the log in your own eye! (Mt 7:3–5) Summing up the nature of hypocrisy in his castigation of certain Pharisees and scribes, Jesus said, "You hypocrites! Well did Isaiah prophesy of you, when he said: 'This people honors me with their lips, but their heart is far from me'" (Mt 15:7–8).

Jesus also expressed his disdain for hypocrisy (the opposite of humility) when he criticized people who "cleanse the outside of the cup and of the plate, but inside they are full of extortion and rapacity." On the occasion when Jesus made that statement he had come under criticism for not washing his hands before eating. I believe that Jesus, as a good Jew and an intelligent person, ordinarily washed his hands before he ate. On that occasion, I think, he intentionally did not wash his hands before he ate because he knew there were people watching him in order to jump on him for any infraction of Jewish custom that he might commit. He wanted to make Micah's point to those people: ritual cleanliness is important, but justice, kindness, and humility are far more important. Washing one's hands but remaining unjust or unkind or arrogant is like washing the outside of a bowl but leaving the inside filthy. Elsewhere he says that a hypocrite is like a whitewashed tomb: pretty on the outside but full of rottenness on the inside (Mt 23:27–28).

Along this same line of *external* compliance with Jewish law but *inward* disregard for it, Jesus criticized people who made a big deal out of supporting the synagogue but "neglected the weightier matters of the law, justice and mercy and faith," thereby laying heavy burdens on people (Lk 11:37–43; notice the parallel to Micah 6:8). "Woe to you lawyers also!" he said, "for you load men with burdens hard to bear, and you yourselves do not touch the burdens with one of your fingers" (Lk 11:45–48). (That, of course, was true of some lawyers then and is true of some lawyers now, but not of all.) Jesus' concern here was for justice and mercy.

Jesus was also outraged that the temple in Jerusalem, the religious center of the Jewish people, was not—as it was supposed to be according to Scripture (Isaiah 56:7)—a house of prayer where the devout could "walk humbly with God." Instead, it was filled with the noise and bustle of money changers and people selling pigeons, sheep, and oxen—in spite of the fact that the prophets emphasized over and over that what God wants from us is justice, kindness, and humility, not burnt offerings (Jn 2:13–17; Isaiah 1:10–17; Amos 5:21–24).

As we have seen, Jesus came under criticism because of his violations of the fourth commandment, which says we should not work on the Sabbath. Some religious dignitaries wanted to punish Jesus for healing people on the Sabbath. Jesus pointed out to those people that they circumcised infant males on the Sabbath. Then he asked them: If it is okay to *circumcise* people on the Sabbath, why is it not also okay to *heal* people on the Sabbath? To permit circumcision on the Sabbath but forbid healing did not seem just or merciful (Jn 7:22–24; Amos 5:21–24; Micah 6:6–8).

Then there is the story of the woman "caught in the very act of committing adultery" (Jn 8:3–11). It is doubtful that the men who brought her to Jesus really cared about adultery. What they were hoping to do was catch Jesus in a contradiction to Mosaic Law so they could arrest him. Hence, they confronted Jesus with the woman and reminded him of the fact that Moses commanded that a woman caught in adultery should be stoned to death. They wanted to know if Jesus agreed with Moses and would condemn the woman to be stoned to death.

Jesus did not express disagreement with Moses. Rather, he bent down and wrote something in the sand. Then he straightened up and said, "Let him who is without sin throw the first stone." Then he bent down and wrote again in the sand. Immediately the dynamics of the situation changed. Apparently without further comment the woman's accusers began leaving "one by one" until all were gone. What deflated the intentions of those men so quickly? I believe it was what Jesus said *plus* what he wrote in the sand.

What did he write? We are not told. But here is a plausible hypothesis. It takes two to commit adultery, but the woman's accusers made no mention of the man who was committing adultery with her when they were caught in the act. The accusers were presenting themselves as righteous, the woman as unrighteous, and were ignoring the man who had been with her. I believe that the first thing Jesus wrote in the sand was "Leviticus 20:10." Then he said, "Let anyone among you who is without sin be the first to throw a stone at her." Then, I believe, for those accusers who did not remember what Leviticus 20:10 said, he wrote it out in the sand. What it said was that according to Moses *the man*, as well as the woman, who commits adultery should be put to death.

Thereby Jesus confronted the injustice of the woman's accusers by asking, in essence, "Where's the man? If you caught her in the act of adultery, then you caught him, too. He, too, is an adulterer. Why didn't you bring him? Are you protecting him? Is he one of you? And which of you has not committed adultery?" Jesus thereby turned the tables on that lynch mob (or in this case, "stone mob"). He reminded them that according to Mosaic Law if they were concerned with justice and not mercy they should have brought the man as well as the woman before Jesus.

Furthermore, maybe not all, but certainly some of the woman's accusers had committed adultery, or had a friend or relative who had done so. Indeed, it's not implausible that catching the woman "*in the very act of adultery*" was only possible because they agreed as to who (perhaps one of them) would commit adultery with her and where and when. Being so deeply involved in this plot, they decided not to put themselves, friends, and relatives at risk of being stoned, so they left quietly, leaving the woman behind with Jesus. Among other things that this story shows is how knowledgeable, sharp, and quick of mind, as well as compassionate, Jesus was. In a tense, dangerous situation he prevented a woman from being stoned to death, he escaped the trap that had been set for him, and he exposed the injustice and cruelty of those who set that trap (Jn 7:53–8.11).

9. CONDEMNED BUT FORGAVE SIN

Jesus loved people but he hated sin. When he dismissed the woman caught in adultery, he told her, "Go and sin no more." At various times Jesus named the following things as sins: theft, murder, fornication, adultery, coveting, wickedness, deceit, licentiousness, envy, slander, bearing false witness, disrespect to parents, pride, and foolishness (Mk 7:21–22 and elsewhere; this is, of course, not an exhaustive list). Jesus emphasized the inward dimension of sin as distinguished from the outward violation of a code of behavior. It is, he said, not what goes into a person's mouth that constitutes sin (all foods are clean); it is the words and actions that come out of a person's heart that constitute sin. That is why Jesus, like the great prophets before him, gave so much attention to attitudes and intentions. It is out of them that words and actions arise.

Jesus was a loving person, but he was tough on sin because he knew the destructiveness of sinful behaviors and attitudes. That's why he was emphatic about the importance of repentance. What does it mean to repent? It means to turn away from sin, inwardly as well as outwardly. Unfortunately, we usually think of repentance only in terms of turning away *from* something—like stealing or lying or adultery or drunkenness. But we cannot turn away from one thing without turning toward something else—and it is just as important that we turn toward something good as that we turn away from something bad. After all, it is possible to turn away from one bad thing to another! That is why Jesus repeatedly emphasized the importance of turning toward the Kingdom of God.

The Kingdom of God is the concept and reality of all that is good. It is that which we should turn toward when we turn away from bad things. The Kingdom of God is, among other things, a dimension of life in which people not only turn away from racism but turn toward friendship between members of different races (I saw a wonderful bumper sticker today. It simply said: "ERACISM".) In turning toward the Kingdom of God we not only turn away from insulting people, we turn toward treating them with dignity; we not only turn away from injuring people but turn toward healing them; we not only turn away from exploiting people but turn toward promoting their well-being; we not only turn away from making strangers feel unwelcome or inferior or invisible but turn toward making them feel welcomed and valued.

If we see the difference between these contrasting things but refuse to repent—to turn away from the bad and toward the good, both in our behavior and in our heart—we are choosing to create and live in a cruel, callous world. Jesus doesn't want us to live there. He wants us to join the party in the Kingdom of God! That is why in blistering terms he condemned the behaviors and attitudes by which we hurt other people and exclude ourselves from the Kingdom of God.

Sin isn't sin simply because God says don't do it. God says "Don't do it!" because it injures people and destroys positive relationships between them. Sin is the party crasher that ruins the fun. It prevents the party from flourishing here on earth. People who are hurt or don't like one another or don't care about one another can't have a happy, ongoing party. Jesus wants to party with us, wants us to party with one another, and wants the party to be eternal, so he hates sin, urges us to turn away from it, and readily forgives us when we turn away from sin and ask to join the party in the Kingdom of God. Heck, he's the one who makes extra wine to ensure that the party keeps going! (Jn 2:1–11)

Jesus affirmed the importance and the power of forgiveness. When we repent—and of course Jesus was speaking of repentance that comes from the heart and not merely from the lips—when we repent, Jesus and his Heavenly Father forgive us. With a smile and a hug we are welcomed to the party! Of course, repentance may call for more than words, even more than heartfelt words. When we can make amends, Jesus said we should do so. He said that if you are about to make an offering to God and remember that someone has something against you, you should "leave your gift there before the altar and go; first be reconciled to your brother or sister, and then come and offer your gift" (Mt 5:23–24). God is happy to wait for us while we do that. God is made happier when we do that. Making amends to others is more precious to God than giving gifts that honor God's name.

And when we repent, Jesus is emphatic that God forgives us. He is equally emphatic that forgiveness is required of us as well as offered to us. That point is made clear in "The Lord's Prayer." In the Lord's Prayer Jesus taught his disciples to ask God, "Forgive us our sins as we forgive those who have sinned against us" (Mt 6:12). (Other translators say "Forgive us our trespasses as we forgive those who have trespassed against us" and "Forgive us our debts as we forgive our debtors.") No matter how that verse is translated, it says clearly that if we repent, God will forgive us—but only if *we* forgive those who ask *us* for forgiveness.

By telling the following dramatic story Jesus illustrated that God's forgiveness of us depends on our forgiveness of others. It seems there was a king who decided to collect the money that his slaves had borrowed from him. One slave owed a lot but could not pay. The king commanded that the slave, together with his wife, children, and all his possessions, be sold to pay his debts. The slave fell on his knees and begged for mercy. The king, moved by compassion, released the slave and cancelled his debts.

Later that slave encountered someone who owed *him* money; he seized the man by the throat, and demanded that he pay up. His debtor, who was also a slave, fell on his knees and begged for mercy, but the slave who had been forgiven threw the other slave into prison until he could pay his debt (which from prison he probably never could repay). When the debtor's friends heard about this, they told the king what happened. The king was outraged. He summoned the first slave and said, "You wicked slave! I forgave you all that debt because you pleaded with me. Should you not have had mercy on your fellow slave, as I had mercy on you?" The king then handed the slave over to be tortured until he paid his entire debt (which he probably never could). "So," Jesus concluded, "my heavenly Father will also do to every one of you, if you do not forgive your brother or sister from your heart" (Mt 18:21–35). In brief, forgiveness is expected of us as well as offered to us.

But what if someone sins against you, you forgive them, and then they sin against you again? If they repent again, do you have to forgive them again? St. Peter asked Jesus this very question. "Lord," he said, "if someone sins against me, how often should I forgive him? As many as seven times?" I suppose seven was the maximum number of times that Peter could imagine forgiving anyone. What did Jesus reply? Did he say, "Yes, seven times"? Or did he raise the ante a little and say "ten times"? No, he said "seventy seven times"! (Mt 18:21–22) That number must have staggered Peter. Peter wanted a rule with a "reasonable" limit to it so he could say to someone: "Okay, buddy, I forgave you seven times, now no more forgiveness!" (One has to wonder where Jesus got the figure of seventy seven times. It does have a biblical background. In Genesis 4:23–24 an early biblical figure, Lamech, says, "If Cain is avenged sevenfold, truly Lamech is avenged seventy-sevenfold." It appears that Jesus was familiar with that statement and was saying that instead of seeking *vengeance* seventy seven fold, we should *forgive* seventy seven fold.)

By contrast to what Peter wanted, Jesus wanted people to focus not on complying with a rule but on becoming a certain kind of person (in this case a forgiving person) (Mt 18:21–22; Lk 17:3–4). Jesus' emphasis on trying to become a certain kind of person, rather than mechanically following a rule, was a point that people often missed. It is part of what is meant by the difference between following "the letter of the law" and living according to "the spirit of the law." Jesus understood and appreciated the difference between the letter of the law and the spirit of the law, between the intent of the law, on the one hand, and a narrow, legalistic way of interpreting the law, on the other hand.

Consider, for example, a Pharisee who went to the temple to pray. As he bragged to God that he did not sin and he gave a tithe to the temple, he sneered at a nearby tax collector, who was full of remorse for his sins. There was no compassion or humility in the Pharisee. He had no sense of his own shortcomings and insensitivities. In Jesus' judgment there was more hope for the remorseful tax collector to enter the Kingdom of God than for the prideful, rule-following Pharisee. Perhaps as Jesus reflected on the difference between those two people he was thinking of Micah's question: "What does the Lord require of you but to do justice, to love mercy, and to walk humbly with him?" (Lk 18:9–14; Micah 6:8)

The ideal of becoming a certain kind of person, rather than just following rules, seems also to have motivated Jesus to tell the story of the Good Samaritan. When Jesus said we should love our neighbor as our self, someone asked, but who is our neighbor? The asker wanted a precise regulation by which he could rule some people in and some people out—a rule by which he could say, "Sorry. You're not my neighbor. I don't have to love you." In the story of the Good Samaritan, Jesus makes clear that what he wants is for us to become people who accept inconveniences and risks to help other people because they need our help—not because we have to follow a rule.

As we close this section on forgiveness, keep in mind that Jesus was not soft on sin. He was an outspoken critic of injustice, hardheartedness, and hypocrisy, and he said that we, also, with appropriate sensitivity and humility, should be critics of such things. "Take heed to yourselves," he said; "if your brother sins, rebuke him, and if he repents, forgive him" (Lk 17:3). Then we can all party happily in the Kingdom of God!

10. JESUS WAS NOT A CHARLATAN

A charlatan is a person who travels about, gathers crowds of people, and makes false claims to have special skill or knowledge in order to manipulate those people for personal gain. Jesus wasn't a charlatan. Crowds followed him, but he didn't try to drum up followers. Indeed, he warned people who followed him that his way was difficult, dangerous, and required wholehearted commitment (Mt 8:18–20). After he healed people he often told them not to tell anyone that he was the one who had cured them. And a close reading of the Gospels reveals no suggestion that he ever asked for or accepted payment of any kind for the good deeds he did. Moreover, when he sent his disciples out to heal the sick, he told them not to accept money for what they did (Mt 10.7–8). He also warned his disciples of the difficulties and dangers of following him. He warned that they would be like lambs in the midst of wolves (Mt 10:16–18). In brief, Jesus never coerced or even threatened anyone to follow him.

When John the Baptist sent his disciples to ask Jesus whether Jesus was "he who is to come," that is, whether Jesus was the Messiah, Jesus didn't give a long oration to convince John's disciples that he was the Messiah, nor did he point to the growing number of people who were following him, nor did he levitate his body or bend an iron spike by staring at it. Rather, he spoke of acts of compassion. He told John's disciples, "Go and tell John what you have seen and heard: the blind receive their sight, the lame walk, the lepers are cleansed, the deaf hear, the dead are raised, the poor have good news brought to them" (Lk 7:18–23). And all free of charge! A charlatan Jesus was not. So gifted, and yet so humble. Amazingly admirable.

11. JESUS WARNED US AGAINST DOOMSDAY PROPHETS

Another reason to admire Jesus is that he tried to protect us from being exploited by doomsday prophets. Doomsday prophets in the Christian tradition claim to know when the world will end (and it will be soon!), or they claim to know that the Messiah has returned to Earth and who he is (and often the prophet says, "C'est moi! It is me!").

The Gospels are clear that Jesus believed in the coming of an end of history, and he spoke of signs of the coming of that time. But the Gospels are equally clear that Jesus was as emphatic as anyone possibly could be that *when* the Christ returns and *who* the Christ is will be so obvious to everyone that no one will have to guess at it or be told by anyone that the end of the world has come or who the Christ is or where he is. In Jesus' own words, "If any one says to you, 'Lo, here is the Christ!' or 'There he is!' do not believe it. For false Christs and false prophets will arise and [note this!] *show great signs and wonders*, so as to lead astray, if possible, even the elect" (my bracket and emphasis). "So," Jesus continues, "if they say to you, 'Lo, he is in the wilderness,' do not go out; if they say, 'Lo, he is in the inner rooms,' do not believe it. For as the lightning comes from the east and shines as far as the west, so will be the coming of the Son of man" (Mt 24:23–28).

When the disciples asked Jesus to tell them *when* the time of universal tribulation would come (the turbulent time right before the end of the world), Jesus said, "Beware that you are not led astray; for many will come in my name and say, 'I am he!' and, 'The time is near!' *Do not go after them*" (Lk 21:8–11; my emphasis). "Of that day and hour *no one knows, not even the angels of heaven, nor the Son*, but the Father only" (Mt 24.36; my emphasis). "Keep awake therefore, for you do not know on what day your Lord is coming" (Mt 24:42). Also, in the first chapter of the book of Acts, Luke reports that on one occasion when Jesus appeared to the disciples after his resurrection, they asked him, "Lord, is this the time when you will restore the kingdom to Israel?" Jesus replied, "It is not for you to know the times or periods that the Father has set by his own authority" (Acts 1:6–7). Hence, according to Jesus there is no need to discuss the date of the end of history or to speculate about it or get worked up about it.

Meanwhile, the thing for us to do, he said, is to live in such a way that when the end comes—whether it be by personal death or the end of history—we will be living in a way that will bring blessings down on us. In Jesus' own words, "Watch therefore, for you do not know on what day your Lord is coming" (Mt 24:42). He also said, "Be on guard so that your hearts are not weighted down with dissipation and drunkenness and the worries of this life, and that day does not catch you unexpectedly, like a trap. For it will come upon all who live on the face of the whole earth." While we are waiting for that day, Jesus added, "Be alert at all times, praying that you may have strength to escape" all the temptations and afflictions that will assault us (Lk 21:34–36). Once again we see that Jesus' emphasis was on *being* a certain kind of person.

It is difficult to believe, but even after Jesus said all that, there are still (and apparently always will be) Christians who claim to know that the end of the world is near and when the end of the world will come or that the Messiah has returned to Earth and who and where he is. It seems pretty obvious that people say such things to fill their bank accounts or gratify their egos or because they are deluded—or maybe they simply haven't read what Jesus said. I think we should admire Jesus for warning us against such people.

12. JESUS DID NOT ABUSE HIS POWER

When I think of power it reminds me of a roaring river. It reminds me of the times I have stood on the edge of Niagara Falls, hearing the roar of the water and feeling the ground tremble under my feet. Power is an awesome, wonderful, and dangerous thing. Jesus had an exquisite sense of what it is appropriate to use power for and of what it is not; of when it is appropriate to use power and when it is not; of how it is appropriate to use power and of how it is not.

Early in this chapter, in the section "Mentally Tough," I pointed out that when Jesus was fasting in the desert immediately before the beginning of his public ministry, he refused to use his power to prove to Satan that he was the Son of God. After his public ministry began, authority figures in Palestine frequently asked him to do the very same thing that the devil had asked, that is, to perform a miracle to prove he was the Messiah. Even on the cross he was taunted by people who told him to come down from the cross if he really was the Son of God. He refused to do so. If he had used his power to do that, it would have destroyed his mission to prove to people that God's love for them is unqualified; the focus of the people would have shifted from Jesus' character and message to his power. Only by Jesus' unconditional love, and therefore his unconditional vulnerability, could the unconditional love of God for humankind be fully expressed and made available. Only by offering himself to the possibility of harsh affliction and a cruel death could Jesus burst the illusion that God's love is conditional, that we must meet God's standards before God will bend to us, that God runs a religious merit system, that God is legalistic not loving.

When Jesus did use his power, when he performed miracles, it was almost always, according to the reports we have, in order to heal people. And when he healed people, he often told them not to tell anyone that he had cured them! Why in the world did he do that? Why didn't he want people to know of his power? Because the purpose of his miracles was not to make a reputation for himself. It was to help the afflicted. To have that kind of power and not abuse it is highly admirable. How much better off the world would be if everyone learned from Jesus what to use power for, and when and how to use it, and what not to use it for, and when and how not to use it.

13. JESUS EMPHASIZED WELL-BEING OVER RULES

Rules are important for living life well, but in unusual circumstances, rules that are normally good may conflict with what is needed. Jesus did not dismiss the importance of rules, but he put the well-being of people ahead of conformity to rules. The rule that seems to have gotten him into the most trouble, as we have seen, was the rule prohibiting work on the Sabbath. Setting aside one day a week for worship, family, and study of Scripture is obviously valuable, but in Jesus' time the interpretation of that commandment excluded almost any effort on the Sabbath except walking to the synagogue to worship, feeding one animals, and feeding oneself (but the food had to be prepared *before* the Sabbath).

One Sabbath when Jesus and his disciples were passing through a corn field and the disciples were hungry, Jesus gave them permission to pick corn and eat it. But picking corn was work, so Jesus got into trouble for making that exception (Lk 6:1–5; Mk 2:27). Curing a person of an affliction, as we have seen, was also considered to be work, and therefore forbidden on the Sabbath. Nonetheless, on a Sabbath Jesus cured a man with a withered hand (Mk 3:1–6) and cured a woman who had been crippled and bent over for eighteen years (Lk 3:15–16). The ruler of the synagogue in which Jesus cured the woman was indignant. He said Jesus should have come on another day to heal her. Jesus replied, in essence: Shame on you, hypocrite. You water your animals on the Sabbath. You pull your sheep out of a pit on the Sabbath (Lk 13:10–17). A person is of much more value than a sheep! (Mt 12:11–12)

Similarly, in John 5:1–16 Jesus cures an invalid, telling him to rise, take up his pallet and waLk But it was the Sabbath, so Jesus got into trouble for curing the man (that was work) and for telling the man to pick up and carry his pallet (which was considered to be work—so Jesus was encouraging someone else to work on the Sabbath). In John 9:1–16 Jesus cures a blind man on the Sabbath by making a clay ointment (work) and putting it on the man's eyes (more work).

Jesus also put human well-being ahead of doctrines about himself, as we see in the following story. On rendezvousing with Jesus after being out and about in the countryside, the disciples told him they had met a man who was casting out demons in Jesus' name but was not one of Jesus' followers. They reported to Jesus that they tried to stop the man, but once again, the disciples "didn't get it." Jesus' concern was to promote the Kingdom of God, the kingdom of compassion, not to promote some kind of orthodoxy about himself. So he told the disciples, "Do not forbid him; for he that is not against you is for you" (Lk 9:49–50).

Finally, consider that magnificent chapter 25 of the Gospel According to Matthew. Therein Jesus says that he and God judge people based on how they treat other people. There is no mention of people being judged on the basis of whether they have been baptized in this way rather than that way, or have a certain understanding of the Atonement, or of the Trinity, etc. That is not to say that these beliefs are unimportant. It is to say that there are things that are even more important. The prophet Micah stated three of those things, which Jesus often referred to: we should act justly, be merciful, and waLk humbly with

God (Micah 6:8). Jesus spelled out some of those priorities more specifically in Matthew 25: we should feed the hungry, give water to the thirsty, clothe the naked, heal the sick, welcome strangers, and visit prisoners. Rule-following and doctrines should be secondary to those priorities.

14. JESUS WAS WISE

Earlier I pointed out that Jesus was very intelligent and quick of mind. But a person can know a lot and be quick of mind without being wise. To be wise is to understand human life and know how to live it well. Jesus was a profoundly wise man. He had a deep understanding of history, human nature, and the influence of circumstances on our behavior and our beliefs. Other people recognized this wisdom in Jesus, so in spite of the fact that he had no formal education and did not come from a scholarly or priestly family, he was often called "teacher" by his followers (The Hebrew word "Rabbi" means "Teacher," so when people called Jesus "Rabbi" they were calling him "Teacher"—which was a term of highest praise in the Jewish community). The Gospels are chock full of wisdom from Jesus—wisdom that can help anyone cope better with life—Christian or non-Christian, believer or non-believer,. Here is a small sample of his insights and teachings (some I will quote; some I will paraphrase):

> Don't undertake a project without first making sure you have the resources to complete it (Lk 14:28–30).

> We should build what is precious on rock, not sand (Mt 7:24–27).
>
> Once you make a thoughtful decision, take action and don't look back (Lk 9:62).
>
> Prepare *now* to take advantage of opportunities when they arise (especially of important, unpredictable, one-time opportunities) (Mt 25:1–13).
>
> Prepare *now* to avoid bad things. Don't let bad events catch you unprepared (Mt 24:42–44).
>
> No one can serve two masters. You will wind up serving the one and hating the other, or hating the one and serving the other. Hence, decide between them! (Lk 16:13)

Life is a serious affair. Actions have consequences. We will be held responsible for our lives, so we should (1) live responsibly and (2) be prepared at all times to be called to account for how we have lived our lives (see Mt 25:14–30, the parable of the talents, and Mt 24:42–44, the parable of the watchful householder).

One of Jesus' most frequently quoted sayings is: "You will know the truth, and the truth will make you free" (Jn 8:32). That statement plus Jesus' emphasis on using our minds has given rise to many of the finest universities in the world, including Harvard and Yale, Notre Dame and Princeton, Oxford and Cambridge, Paris and Heidelberg.

Another of Jesus' most quoted sayings is this: "It is more blessed to give than to receive" (Acts 20:35). Modern psychology has confirmed the truth of this over and over.

Jesus also said, "Stay awake and pray that you may not come into the time of temptation; the spirit indeed is willing, but the flesh is weak" (Mt 26:41). Jesus had a keen understanding of the power of temptation to weaken our strength of will, to undermine our good intentions, to deflect us from our goals, to generate rationalizations and excuses, to distort the way we feel and what we think is important. Hence, it is not surprising that when his disciples asked him to teach them a prayer, he taught them to ask the Heavenly Father: "lead us not into temptation."

Before turning to another topic, I hasten to add that much of Jesus' wisdom is conveyed in *stories* that he told, rather than in brief sayings. Consider, for example, the parables of the rich fool (Lk 12:13–21), the prodigal son (Lk 15:11–32), and the unjust steward (Lk 16:1–13).

Finally, here is perhaps an example of something wise that Jesus *did* rather than *said*. I have in mind the story of Jesus' feeding of several thousand people with five loaves of bread and two fish (Mt 14:13–21; Mk 6:32–44; Lk 9:10–17; Jn 6:1–14). This is a story according to which Jesus caused a very small amount of food to feed several thousand people and leave several baskets of leftovers. An important thing to consider here is that there are different kinds of miracles. It is usually assumed that the miracle that Jesus performed was to multiply those two fish and five loaves like a magician pulling rabbit after rabbit out of a hat—only in this case it would have been pulling fish after fish and loaf after loaf out of a basket. That may be the way it happened, and that would demonstrate the *power* of Jesus, but there is another possibility that would demonstrate the *wisdom* of Jesus rather than his power.

The background to the story is that thousands of people had followed Jesus into a remote area to hear his wisdom. As the day began to wane, Jesus' disciples urged him to send the people away so the people could find food for themselves. To the astonishment of the disciples, Jesus didn't send the crowd away. Instead he told the disciples, "You give them food." The disciples were flabbergasted. They told Jesus they didn't have near enough money to buy food for such a crowd, and that the only food they knew of were five loaves of bread and two fish that a boy in the crowd was willing to give them—which was far from enough to feed a multitude.

What Jesus was wise enough to know, and the disciples failed to consider, I propose, was that the people who had followed Jesus were not stupid or inexperienced. They knew that going out to see Jesus would be an all-day affair, so most of them had taken an appropriate amount of food and drink, as if going on a daylong hike. But each individual, couple, or family was looking out for itself alone; they kept their provisions concealed from others, so it was not evident that they had food with them—or at least not evident how much they had.

Jesus told the crowd that he knew they were hungry, as were he and the disciples, but that the only food he had to offer were only five loaves of bread and two fish that had been offered to him by a boy in the crowd. It wasn't much, he told them, but it was something, so he would share it with them. Then he gave thanks to God and passed the loaves and fish to the people. It was evident to the crowd that Jesus was giving to them the only food that he, the disciples, and the boy had. That's when the miracle began. The boy's generosity and Jesus' generosity melted the hearts of the people and caused them to bring out their own food, so they each took a pinch of what Jesus had passed to them, added some of their own food to it, and passed it along so that everyone, including Jesus and the disciples, would have something to eat. It turned out that the people, in their own wisdom, had brought along so much food that at the end of this love feast, twelve baskets of leftovers were gathered!

It is important to realize that there are different kinds of miracles. There is the cure of someone whose condition is medically hopeless; there is the survival of the person who should have died in a terrible accident; there is the birth of a baby; there is the beauty of a flower, there is the transformation of a self-centered, stingy person to an other-centered, generous person (like Ebenezer Scrooge in Charles Dickens' *A Christmas Carol*). The feeding of the multitude may have been a miracle of this latter kind. If it was, what a dramatic and wonderful thing it was for all those people to shift from clutching their food for their own consumption to passing it along to make sure that everyone got something to eat before they had to start on their long trek back home.

After Jesus performed this miracle of transformation, St. John says that the people began advancing toward him to make him their king! If the miracle was not what I have suggested but was, rather, a magical multiplication of the loaves and fishes, then a plausible interpretation of the multitude's motivation is that they were thinking, "If Jesus can turn a little food into a lot of food, then he's the guy we want for king. With Jesus as king we will never go hungry!" But if the miracle that Jesus performed was to transform a crowd of self-centered, distrustful individuals into a community of concerned, generous neighbors, then a more flattering interpretation of the motivation of the crowd is that they were enormously touched and impressed that Jesus could change their hearts of stone into hearts of flesh, unifying them and motivating them to share with one another. I think that's why they wanted him to be their king—because they had witnessed an enormous miracle of the heart—a miracle that was rooted in Jesus' exquisite wisdom.

15. JESUS ENCOURAGED USE OF REASON

Now let's turn to another reason for admiring Jesus. When a Pharisee asked Jesus, "Teacher, which commandment in the law is the greatest?" Jesus replied, "You shall love the Lord your God with all your heart, and with all your soul, *and with all your mind.* This is the greatest and first commandment" (Mt 22:35–38; Mk 12:28–31; Lk 10:25–27; my emphasis). Jesus' response to the Pharisee's question means we should *think* long, deep, and hard about the existence of God, the nature of God, the will of God, and God's relation to the world. We should *ask* the questions that occur to us, not shy away from them because they might seem sacrilegious. We should question what doesn't make sense to us or doesn't seem to be true. That's how we honor the mind that God gave us. Surely God gave us our minds to be used! When we accept things on blind faith, we are violating what Jesus taught; we are ignoring the God-given purpose of our minds, and we are making ourselves easy pickings for religious frauds and fanatics (against whom Jesus warned us—remember reason number 8 to admire Jesus?).

On a more specific topic, Jesus warned that after his death there would be "false prophets, who come to you in sheep's clothing but inwardly are ravenous wolves" (Mt 7:15–20). Hence, he urged that we should use our God-given minds to make sure we don't follow a false prophet. How can we distinguish true prophets from false prophets? Not by who they say they are or by what they say they believe or by how many followers they have. Rather, Jesus said, "You shall know them by their fruits" (Mt 7:16). The fruits of which he spoke are *deeds* of justice, compassion, and friendship (Mt 25:31–46), as can be seen clearly in the following story.

When John the Baptist sent his disciples to ask Jesus whether he was the Messiah, Jesus said, in effect, "Don't try to determine whether someone is the Messiah by *asking* him if he is. Look at what that person has *done* and *is doing*. Judge from that!" (Mt 11:1–6) Did Jesus make an exception of himself? Did he say we should examine others *but not him*? Not at all! He challenged his closest followers with the following question, "Who do *you* say I am?" (Mt 16:13–15) He was encouraging them to *think* about that question. And he means for us, too, to think about that question. We will return to this point in Chapter 5 when I discuss reasons why people doubt Jesus. But before we do, consider the following.

A careful reading of the first three Gospels (Matthew, Mark, and Luke) makes it clear that Jesus wanted people to think for themselves. Jesus was not a teacher in the modern sense of a lecturer who tells people what to think about his or her area of expertise. Jesus gave people plenty to think about, but he almost never told people *what* to think. Rather, he told parables that caused people to think.

Evidence of this is that some times after Jesus told a parable to a crowd, the disciples later, in private, had to ask Jesus to tell them what the parable meant. Jesus had not told the crowds, including the disciples, what he meant by his stories and parables. Moreover, sometimes when people asked Jesus for answers, he refused to answer. Other times *he* was the one who asked the questions, as we saw above in reason 4.

Consider also the fact that Jesus' favorite teaching tool was the parable. Parables don't provide answers—at least not in an obvious way. They point out a similarity between two things or tell a story that makes our minds begin whirring. Some parables use a brief analogy. For example, "The kingdom of heaven is like yeast that a woman took and mixed with three measures of flour until all of it was leavened" (Mt 13:33). Exactly how does THAT tell us what the kingdom of heaven is like? And what IS the kingdom of heaven? Jesus doesn't say explicitly. Other parables tell a story; for example, the parable of the prodigal son (Lk 15:11–32). Exactly what are we to think of the "good" son who stayed home? Why is that even in the story?

Until recently, whenever I thought of Jesus speaking to crowds, I pictured a rapt audience that listened quietly and departed reverently. Now I don't think that way. Jesus spoke to crowds of common people who were used to boisterous interactions. I think Jesus interacted with his listeners. I think his analogies, metaphors, and stories were intended to arouse thoughtful responses, discussion, and debate, and I believe that vigorous discussion of Jesus' parables continued among his listeners long after they left his presence.

By means of his aphorisms, analogies, and stories Jesus was a great teacher. Indeed, "teacher" is the most common title that people give to him in the New Testament. As a teacher Jesus was like the great Greek philosopher Socrates. Socrates provoked people into thinking by asking them questions—by asking them to explain or justify what they said. Jesus provoked people into thinking by telling parables. Sadly, Jesus and Socrates were both executed for getting under the skins of powerful people. They both deserve our profound admiration for speaking truth to powerful people and encouraging us to think for ourselves.

To summarize the results of this chapter, Jesus is worthy of our admiration because, among other things, he was (1) physically tough, (2) mentally tough, (3) highly intelligent, (4) mentally quick, (5) independent, and (6) courageous, plus he (7) hated hypocrisy, (8) emphasized justice, mercy, and humility, (9) forgave but condemned sin, (10) was not a charlatan, (11) warned us against doomsday prophets, (12) did not abuse his awesome gifts, (13) emphasized well-being over rules, (14) was wise, and (15) encouraged us to use our minds in religious matters.

2

Reasons to Love Jesus

IF YOU DOUBTED BEFORE, I hope you are now convinced that Jesus is worthy of great admiration. In this chapter I will set forth reasons for loving him.

1. WOMEN

In chapter 1, reason 1, I argued that Jesus was "a man's man." But this was only one facet of that amazingly complex human. Just as Jesus loved and respected men, and they loved and respected him, Jesus loved and respected women, and they loved and respected him. For example, we are told that women as well as men followed Jesus as he went through the cities and villages of Judea "preaching and bringing the good news of the Kingdom of God" (Lk8:1–3). Moreover, we are told that at the end of his life, in addition to the men who were present at his crucifixion in Jerusalem, "There were also many women there, looking on from afar, who had followed Jesus from Galilee, ministering to him" (Mt 27:55). That means those women traveled many miles by foot or by donkey to be with Jesus and take care of him in his time of trial and suffering.

An example of why women loved him can seen in the following story. When Martha complained on one occasion that her sister Mary was sitting at Jesus' feet with the men, listening to Jesus rather than helping prepare the evening meal, Jesus didn't tell Mary to go help Martha. Rather, he invited Martha to sit down and join them. Jesus lived in a male dominated society, but he didn't treat women in a domineering way.

Or did he? There is a story that might make Jesus seem sexist, so let's examine it. The Gospels of Matthew, Mark, and Luke all tell us that one time when Jesus went to Peter's house, Peter's mother-in-law was "lying sick with a fever." The story says that Jesus banished the fever, and then Peter's mother-in-law rose and served them. It might be thought that Jesus cured her so she could serve them, but in that story Jesus didn't tell her to serve them. There isn't even a suggestion that he hinted that she do so. Serving Jesus was apparently something that *she* wanted to do (Mt 8:14–15; Mk 1:29–31; Lk 4:38–39). Consider also that Jesus told his male disciples to be servants of others—not to sit around expecting others to serve them (Mt 20:26–28).

Then there are stories of Jesus healing sick and afflicted women. For example, he healed a woman who had had a hemorrhage for twelve years (Mk 5:25–34), and there were other women whom he "cured of evil spirits and infirmities." Among the latter was Mary Magdalene, from whom Jesus is said to have cast out seven demons (Lk:8.1–3). (The most important thing here is not whether Mary's problem was demons or something that medical science today would describe in a very different way; the important thing is that she was afflicted and Jesus helped her.)

That Jesus helped these women is one more reason to think he was motivated by love rather than personal gain. Because of their lowly status in ancient Palestine there was little, if anything, for Jesus to gain from healing those women. Moreover, it is clear that many of the women he cured were poor and could not reward him, or they were old and could not follow him, but he cured them anyway.

Here is another interesting account of Jesus' attitude toward women. Even today men try to avoid describing themselves in terms that are associated with women, and men often bristle when described in feminine terms. Such statements as "You are a sissy," "You throw like a girl," "You look like a woman," are usually intended as insults. That attitude is beginning to change as athletic competition has opened up to women, and some women have proven to be more competitive and able than many men. Things were not so in Jesus' time, yet he did not shy from describing himself in female terms. During his last visit to Jerusalem, in one of the most touching scenes in the Gospels, Jesus looked at that great city on a hill and said, "Jerusalem, Jerusalem, the city that kills the prophets and stones those who are sent to it! How often have I desired to gather your children together as a hen gathers her brood under her wings, and you were not willing" (Mt 23:37). In that heart felt statement Jesus compared himself not to a strutting rooster or some other male creature, but to a female creature, a motherly hen. That was the image that captured best the way he was feeling and what he wanted to say.

Jesus also shielded women from abuse. Before he went to Jerusalem for the last time, a group of scribes and

Pharisees, as we saw earlier, brought before Jesus a woman who had been caught in the act of adultery. They were obviously trying to manipulate Jesus into giving a response that would discredit him. Others had tried to do this and failed. I can imagine these men brainstorming: "This didn't work. That didn't work. Hey, I know a woman who will engage in adultery. Let's catch her in the act, take her before Jesus, and ask him whether he agrees with Moses that she should be stoned to death. Let's see him wriggle out of that!"

But Jesus didn't wriggle; he escaped the point of their attack by turning it against them. He didn't condemn the woman or absolve the men who exploited her. Rather, as we saw earlier, he protected the woman by asking, in essence, "Where's the *man* who committed adultery with her? Moses said that the man should be stoned, too!" (Lev.20:10) That cooled off the crowd, since certainly some of *them* had committed adultery, or they had a friend or relative who had, so they decided to leave quietly rather than run the risk of exposing themselves or their male friends and relatives to the possibility of being stoned (Jn 7:53—8:11).

In addition to the preceding story there is another in which Jesus defends a woman and chides the men who fault her. Like the story in which Jesus compared himself to a mother hen, this story takes place after Jesus has gone to Jerusalem for the last time—a time during which, we are told, "The chief priests and the scribes were looking for a way to arrest Jesus by stealth and kill him." Mark tells us that while Jesus and some of the disciples were at Bethany in the house of Simon the Leper, just outside Jerusalem, as Jesus sat at a table, "a woman came with an alabaster jar of very costly ointment of nard, and she broke open the jar and poured the ointment on his head. But some disciples were there who said to one another in anger, 'Why was the ointment wasted in this way? This ointment could have been sold for more than three hundred denarii, and the money given to the poor.' And they scolded her. But Jesus said, 'Let her alone; why do you trouble her? She has performed a good service for me. For you always have the poor with you, and you can show kindness to them whenever you wish; but you will not always have me. She has done what she could; she has anointed my body beforehand for its burial. Truly I tell you, wherever the good news is proclaimed in the whole world, what she has done will be told in remembrance of her.'" And so it has been—it just happened again in my telling of the story! In some translations Jesus told the disciples that the woman had done "a beautiful thing." In brief, some of the men chided the woman, but Jesus chided the men, affirmed her, and explained her loving thoughtfulness in a way that still touches us 2000 years later (see Mk 14:1–9).

Jesus' regard for women and his disregard for opinion that showed disrespect for women is illustrated further in John 4:1–30. A serious disagreement had arisen among the Israelites long before Jesus' time, and it resulted in a split between the Jews and the Samaritans—the Jews being based in southern and northern Palestine (Judea and Galilee, respectively) and the Samaritans in between them in Samaria. Many Jews and Samaritans despised one another and refused to have anything to do with one another. Keeping these facts in mind will help us appreciate more keenly the following story.

On a trip through Samaria, Jesus became fatigued and stopped at a famous well (the well of the patriarch Jacob). "A Samaritan woman came to draw water [from the well], and Jesus [who was by himself] said to her, 'Give me a drink.' [Jesus' disciples had gone to a nearby city to buy food, and he had no way to draw water from the well.] The Samaritan woman said to him, 'How is it that you, a Jew, ask a drink of me, a woman of Samaria?'" The woman was puzzled—perhaps suspicious or cynical—that a Jewish man would ask her for a drink of water. This just was not done! A fascinating conversation ensued between Jesus and the woman. Then the disciples returned from their trip to buy food and "were astonished that [Jesus] was speaking with a woman." It is amusing how many times the disciples were shocked by Jesus' statements or actions. One of the things that turned their world upside down was Jesus' respect for women. (To read the preceding story see Jn 4:1–30.)

For a final point about why women love Jesus (and why we should love him) I turn to an observation by William Craig, as reported in Lee Strobel's book, *The Case for Christ* (Grand Rapids, MI: Zondervan Publishing House, 1998). We have already noted that, in general, women were low on the ladder of respect and authority in Jesus' society. Craig's more specific point is that women were not sufficiently respected to be allowed to be legal witnesses in trials—no matter how much they knew about the issue being examined. Jesus revolutionized that situation by appearing to women *before* appearing to men after his resurrection. All four Gospels agree that the resurrected Jesus appeared to women first; then the women reported to the men, and although the men did not believe them until Jesus also appeared to them, when he did appear to them, that meant the men henceforth had to respect the women's testimony and accept them as competent, important witnesses—which made for a quantum leap forward in their social status.

As Craig argues, if it were not true that Jesus appeared to women first, the men who wrote the Gospels would not have said so, as it was no doubt discomforting to them that they weren't the ones to whom Jesus appeared first. It is reported that during Jesus' time there were ancient rabbinical sayings such as, "Let the words of the Law [of Moses] be burned rather than delivered to women" and "Blessed is he whose children are male, but woe to him whose children are female" (Strobel, 293). Hence, Jesus' acceptance of and respect for women was radically different from common practice, and it was radical that after his resurrection he took a dramatic step that henceforth, at least within the church, secured the competence of women to be legal witnesses.

2. CHILDREN

Jesus loved children. Mothers trusted him with their children. They wanted Jesus to hold their children, talk to them, and bless them. As Matthew says, mothers took their children, even their infants, to Jesus "that he might touch them, lay his hands on them and pray." On one occasion the disciples sternly told some mothers to go away and not bother Jesus with their children. When Jesus saw what the disciples were doing, he was indignant. He rebuked the disciples, and then, says Luke, Jesus called the children to him, saying, "Let the children come to me, and do not hinder them; for to such belongs the kingdom of God." I can just see the children—having been shooed away, perhaps even intimidated by the disciples—running to Jesus in glee when he summoned them. Then, Mark tells us, "He took them in his arms and blessed them, laying his hands upon them." What a tender, touching scene—especially considering that Jesus knew he would soon die and never have children of his own (See Mt 19:13–15, Mk 10:13–16, Lk18:15–17).

On an earlier occasion Jesus issued a harsh warning against anyone who would harm a child: "Whoever causes one of these little ones who believe in me to sin," he said, "it would be better for him to have a great millstone fastened round his neck and to be drowned in the depth of the sea" (Mt 18:6–9). In the next verse Jesus adds, "See that you do not despise one of these little ones; for I tell you that in heaven their angels always behold the face of my Father who is in heaven." I'm not sure how to understand what he meant by "their angels," but it is clear that Jesus thought that children are precious to the Heavenly Father and should also be precious to us.

Finally, when the disciples turned to Jesus to settle a quarrel as to who would be greatest in the kingdom of heaven, we are told that he "took a child, and put him in the midst of them; and taking him in his arms, he said to the disciples, 'Truly, I say to you, whoever does not receive the kingdom of God like a child shall not enter it.'" Then he added, "Whoever receives one such child in my name receives me; and whoever receives me, receives not me but him who sent me." What a profound condemnation of child abuse; what a profound exaltation of child care! How can we help but love such a person? Moreover, I think it is significant that there was a child nearby for Jesus to use to make his point. Children were often around Jesus because they were members of the families of Jesus' followers and because, as we have seen, parents brought their children to be blessed or healed by him (Mk 9:33–37).

3. VOLUNTARY SUFFERING FOR OTHERS

Over and over Jesus took extra steps—literally as well as figuratively—to help people in need. Earlier we heard of him giving away food to a crowd of people so they wouldn't be hungry. Also, he walked from village to village to spread good news about God, to befriend people, give them hope, help them believe in themselves, and heal them. (And even if all of Jesus' healings were brought about only by psychological influence, psychosomatic healings are real, too. Ask any physician.)

Jesus did all of this without charging a cent. That seems to be why he was surprised by the rejection he met in his home town, Nazareth (Mk 6:4–6). There he was not able to do great works to benefit the people because even though he asked nothing from them except that they accept his good will, they would not do it. And that seems to be the key to Jesus' ministry. He stands ready to help if we simply accept him and let him do his work. But without that acceptance, he cannot enter and "do great works."

Finally I mention his greatest voluntary suffering: his acceptance of the contempt, abuse, torture, and crucifixion to which he knew his exposure of hypocrisy, his condemnation of injustice, and his violation of custom on behalf of compassion would lead.

4. HAPPINESS

Jesus was no ascetic. He believed in happiness. He had many friends and enjoyed the good things of this life. When he invited Levi the tax collector to become one of his followers, what did Levi do? He didn't put on sack cloth and a long face. He happily accepted Jesus' invitation and invited many people to his home for a celebration. As Luke puts it, Levi gave "a great banquet" for Jesus (Lk 5:29). Banquets are happy occasions: good food, good drink, good fellowship, good times.

Weddings, too, were happy occasions in Jesus' time, as in ours. Perhaps the happiest part of a wedding in Jesus' time was the banquet after the wedding. So when Jesus wanted to impress on his listeners how wonderful the kingdom of heaven is, he said, "The kingdom of heaven may be compared to a king who gave a wedding banquet for his son" (Mt 22:1–3). One of the earliest stories in the Gospel of John is of Jesus at a wedding party. Jesus didn't merely go to the party. He helped keep the party going by making more wine when the host ran out! (Jesus' mother, Mary, deserves a point for an assist because she was the one who asked him to take care of the problem. Apparently Mary, too, appreciated the social value of wine.) (John 2:1–11)

If Jesus had been opposed to drinking wine, he could have said to his mother, "Let'em drink water!" Some might say that Jesus made wine because water wasn't safe in those times, but if Jesus was opposed to drinking alcohol, he could have just made water that was safe (if he could turn water into wine, he certainly could have made water that was safe to drink!). Or he could have made non-alcoholic wine. There is, however, no suggestion that that's what he did.

At Levi's banquet for Jesus we learn that Jesus knew the difference between good wine and mediocre or bad wine. "No one," he said, "after drinking old wine desires new wine." Rather, he said, the person who has drunk well-aged wine says, "The old is good" (I can just imagine Jesus saying, "The old is Goo*ood*!" and laughing) (Lk5:39). Jesus not only knew what good wine was, he appreciated it. When he made wine at the wedding feast at which the host ran out of wine, he didn't make bad wine or mediocre wine in order to discourage people from drinking more. Rather, he made wine that the wine steward said was the best that had been served at the party! Finally, as though to emphasize the value of wine and the importance of Jesus having changed water to wine, when Jesus returned to Cana on a later occasion, the Gospel According to John says this: "So he came again to Cana in Galilee, where he had made the water wine" (Jn 4:46). St. John obviously thought that was an occasion that should not be forgotten.

Moreover, Jesus didn't just make wine; he drank it. Most famously he drank wine at his last supper with his disciples before his arrest and crucifixion. If he was opposed to alcohol he could have insisted on water at the last supper. If only wine was available, he could have changed the wine into water. But he didn't. Indeed, at the last supper Jesus took a cup of wine, *passed it to his disciples* and said, "As often as you drink it . . . do it in remembrance of me." Do what in remembrance of him? Drink wine! (I Cor.11:23–25; my emphasis) Finally, Jesus told his disciples at the last supper that although he would not drink wine with them for awhile, some day he would drink wine with them again. Where? "In my Father's kingdom" (Mt 26:29). As we earlier heard Jesus say, the Kingdom of God is like a wedding party—a wedding party at which good wine is served.

Before moving to other indications that Jesus believed in having a good time, I want to emphasize that the Bible is full of injunctions against drunkenness, and I am keenly aware that drinking alcohol can cause serious problems, even tragedies. However, so can many other things when not done in moderation or when done by people who cannot do them in moderation. In spite of those risks, the Bible does not contain injunctions against drinking wine, but it does contain praise of the gladness that wine brings when drunk in moderation.

Continuing on the theme of Jesus' belief in happiness, let's return to Jesus' emphasis on the Kingdom of God. It was during Levi's "great banquet" for Jesus that some Pharisees and scribes challenged Jesus by referring to John the Baptist and saying, "John's disciples, like the disciples of the Pharisees, frequently fast and pray, but your disciples eat and drink." Jesus replied, "You cannot make wedding guests fast while the bridegroom is with them, can you?" Remember, weddings are joyous occasions: the marriage ceremony itself is joyous, and then there are festivities after the ceremony. As long as the bridegroom and the bride stay around, the party continues. In his reply to the Pharisees and scribes Jesus was comparing himself to the bridegroom and saying that while he, Jesus, is with us it is time for feeling good—while he was with us in the flesh, while he is with us through the Holy Spirit, and when he will be with us in the Kingdom of Heaven. Hence, lovers of Jesus shouldn't fast and mourn when the bridegroom is with them (Lk 5:34–39). And don't forget, Jesus said: whenever two or three are gathered in his name, there he is with them!

Elsewhere Jesus said the Kingdom of God is like a great banquet to which everyone is invited: the wealthy and the poor, the healthy and the ill, the athletic and the lame, the whole and the maimed, the seeing and the blind, etc. A sad, puzzling thing is that many people don't want to go to the party, and they keep other people out by promoting suspicion, cynicism, fear, greed, jealousy, and anger. Perhaps that is why Jesus wept at the sight of Jerusalem as he entered it for the last time. He wanted to have a party, but Jerusalem did not.

Jerusalem was a real city, of course, but it was also symbolic. It was symbolic of all cities and societies that ignore or reject the things that would allow us to party eternally—to enjoy being with one another and God (Mt 26:29). But to his followers Jesus said: Someday I will drink wine with you again—"in my Father's kingdom"! And according to the Gospel of Luke, Jesus told his disciples, "You are those who have continued with me in my trials; as my Father appointed a kingdom for me, so do I appoint for you that you may eat and drink at my table in my kingdom" (Lk22:28–30). So according to Jesus there will be a party in the everlasting kingdom of God, and we can begin to participate in it even now.

Finally, we all know that Jesus underwent great suffering, but his suffering was for the sake of joy. His suffering was surrounded on both ends of his life by joy. Jesus' life on earth began on a note of joy, continued on a note of joy, then was interrupted by a period of horror, then was climaxed on a note of joy. According to Luke 2:10, when Jesus was born, an angel announced to nearby shepherds, "Fear not; for behold, I bring you tidings of great joy!" That message was followed by joyous music from a heavenly host. During Jesus' life he emphasized that he had come to bring peace and joy to us. Speaking of his followers he said, "I came that they may have life, and have it abundantly. I am the good shepherd. The good shepherd lays down his life for the sheep" (Jn 10:10–11). That statement beautifully ties together two fundamental themes of Jesus' life: his belief in happiness and his voluntary suffering for our happiness. Later in John's Gospel Jesus says to his disciples, "I have said these things to you so that my joy may be in you, and that your joy may be complete" (Jn 15:11). Obviously, Jesus wanted us to be happy, and I love him for that.

5. HUMOR

Jesus was funny. I don't mean funny in the sense of odd or eccentric. I mean he said things that must have made people smile or laugh (some of his statements certainly affect me that way). He appreciated humor and used it to good effect. His teachings and stories are full of amusing analogies. For example, knowing that salt preserved food and made it taste better, and wanting his followers to be people who preserve good things and make life "taste better," Jesus told his disciples to be "the salt of the earth" (note again his emphasis on *being* a certain kind of person). So far not funny, right? But then he told his disciples to be sure to *keep* themselves salty; because, he said, if salt *loses* its saltiness, how are you going to restore its saltiness? Put salt on it??? No, he said; if salt loses its saltiness, it becomes worthless, good for nothing, and might as well be thrown away. Moral of the analogy? Be the salt of the earth—and be sure to keep yourself salty! (Mt 5:13; Mk 9:50; Lk 14:34–35)

In another analogy Jesus linked light with good, and darkness with evil, and urged his followers to be "the light of the world." "Let your light shine before others," he told them, "so that they may see your good works and give glory to your Father in heaven." After all, Jesus said, if it is dark and you want to light up the house, you don't light a candle and then put it under a bowl or a basket, where it wouldn't be visible, or under a bed, which would catch on fire. Though that would certainly light things up! And, he added, you wouldn't put your candle down in the basement when the people who need light are upstairs! (Mt 5:14–16; Lk 8:16; Mk 4:21)

Then, as we saw earlier, there is what Jesus said about judgmental people. Using logs and specks to compare different sizes of faults, Jesus said that judgmental people have *logs* stuck in their own eyes, but all they see are the specks in other people's eyes! (That would make a great cartoon using logs and toothpicks or logs and specks of sawdust.) (Mt 7:3–5)

For a final example of Jesus' use of humor, consider his use of different analogies to make the same point to different audiences: women and men. The single point of the analogies, roughly speaking, is that new things can't be forced into old categories without causing a problem. Jesus illustrated this point to women by an analogy that was intimately familiar to them and no doubt amused them. You don't mend an old garment, he said, by sewing a new piece of fabric into it. As women knew, if you did that, then when the garment was washed, the old material in the garment would stay the same size because it had shrunk in previous washings, but the new fabric would shrink and thereby tear away from the old fabric, making the garment worse instead of better.

To men Jesus made the same point by saying, in essence, "You know what will happen if you put new wine into old wineskins. The old wineskins have dried and lost their flexibility, so if you put new wine into them, the new wine will ferment and expand until it bursts the old wineskins, causing the wine to spill out and be lost." What a silly thing that would be to do! (Perhaps a contemporary parallel would be thinking you can keep carbonated soda in a styrofoam cup by just sticking a plastic lid on it even though the cup is going to get bounced around. Who has not made that mistake? Or am I the only one?)

6. FRIENDSHIP

Jesus believed in friendship. The apostles, the sisters Mary and Martha, and their brother Lazarus were all very dear to him (Jn 11:1–44; 19:25–27). In John 15:12–15 Jesus explains to the disciples that he is their friend and that they are his friends. "This is my commandment," he said to them, "that you love one another as I have loved you. No one has greater love than this, to lay down one's life for one's friends. You are my friends if you do what I command you." Obviously, friendship was very important to Jesus. That truth is captured in a popular hymn that begins by saying, "What a friend we have in Jesus."

Also, there are touching scenes that occurred during Jesus' last meal with his disciples before he was arrested.

Especially moving to me is the following part of the Last Supper. After Jesus blessed the bread and wine and told the disciples to eat and drink of them, he said, "Do this in remembrance of me." Jesus knew that was his last meal with them and that he would be dead soon. He was saying to his beloved disciples, "Dear friends, please do not forget me. When you eat bread and drink wine with one another, use it as an occasion to remember me—please." I think he probably said "Do this in remembrance of me" while looking tenderly into their eyes, perhaps with tears in his (I Cor.11:23–26).

Orthodox doctrine is that Jesus was fully human as well as fully God. As a human Jesus would not have known that he would rise again after his death. He could have had faith that he would and could have hoped that he would, but, as St. Paul pointed out, faith and hope fall short of knowledge. So I believe there was real pathos in Jesus' request that his friends remember him—just as there was pathos in his prayer in the Garden of Gethsemane when he asked that God deliver him from being crucified. Jesus' Gethsemane prayer made it clear that as a human he did not know for certain whether he would be crucified, but he knew it was highly probable unless God intervened—and he hoped God would.

7. THE REALITY AND IMMORTALITY OF EACH INDIVIDUAL

Atheists typically believe that when a person dies, he or she ceases to exist forever. Some religious people believe the same thing. For example, not all people in Jesus' time believed in life after death. An important group of Jews, the Sadducees, did not believe in life after death (Mt 22:23–33; Acts 23:1–8). Some Asian religions teach that individual personality is an inferior form of existence that is only temporary. Eventually, they say, we will transcend our individual personalities and enter into a higher, non-personal level of existence which will consist of pure bliss but no awareness of self or others (because there will be no self or others). Other religions say that the appearance of there being a multitude of separate persons in this life or beyond this life is an illusion. In truth there is only the One, and the One is beyond all categories. It is, they say, a bit like being in a house of mirrors that multiplies and distorts your reflection in many mirrors simultaneously, making it look like there are many people present when there is only you. According to this philosophy, at death the illusion of multiplicity is left behind as we merge into the all-encompassing One, like bubbles of sea-spray merging back into the ocean.

Jesus had a point of view that was very different from the preceding positions. He believed that individual persons are real, precious, and, by the will of God, immortal. In addition to believing that we are immortal and distinct from one another, Jesus believed that we are made for eternal friendship: God with us and us with God; and us with one another. It is from that point of view that Jesus gave us hope for reunion after death with those we love and admire in this life. He did not dismiss, devalue, or believe in the destruction of personal life.

Before his crucifixion Jesus told his disciples they were his friends and that he soon would die but that one day, in the Kingdom of God, they would all be together again. The next day when he was still alive but nailed to a cross, being harassed and cursed by a jeering crowd, a thief who was crucified next to him did a staggeringly kind thing. I don't think the thief believed that Jesus was the Messiah, but he heard people mocking Jesus for claiming to be the Messiah. The thief sensed Jesus' innocence and goodness, and he detested the vicious abuse that was being heaped on him, so he tried to comfort Jesus by saying, "Jesus, remember me when you come into your kingdom."

Jesus, in response, did not try to comfort the thief in the way that an atheist or a Sadducee might, by telling him that soon they would both cease to exist forever and no longer be in pain. Rather, he said to the thief, "Truly I tell you, today you will be with me in Paradise." In that simple statement Jesus affirmed both the preciousness and the immortality of that man. What incredible acts of love the thief and Jesus showed to each other while they were suffering terribly and so close to death. How can we help but hope that Jesus was right and that the compassionate thief soon got a wonderful surprise by finding himself in Paradise with Jesus? (Lk 23:32–43) How can we help but love someone who gives us such hope?

8. JESUS, THE GREAT PHYSICIAN

Jesus is known as "the great physician." The Gospels say that he cured the sick, the blind, the mute, the lame, the maimed, and the emotionally afflicted. He healed people "with various diseases and pains, demoniacs, epileptics, and paralytics" (Mt 4:24). He cured people who were hemorrhaging; he cured people with dropsy and leprosy. Some of those people were considered in Jesus' society to be unclean and untouchable. They were shunned, rejected, treated with fear and loathing. But Jesus reached out to them and even touched them so he could heal them. He never asked or took compensation for those healings. He performed them out of compassion for suffering humanity.

Some people think that these purported cures either did not take place or were exaggerated or were coincidence. To them I say that we need to make a distinction between two questions: the question as to whether Jesus performed miracles and the question as to the significance *for us* of the stories about Jesus performing miracles. What is important for us, I think, is the example Jesus set for us: an example of caring about and doing something about the misery of others. We should do likewise by, for example, engaging in or supporting medical research and the application of medicine to human needs. Should we pray for miracles? Yes. By all means! But meanwhile we should also work for a cure with the minds and hands God gave us.

What is most important for us is to share Jesus' ministry of healing in whatever ways we can. Medical research and the practice of medicine—as carried out by physicians, nurses, therapists, social workers, lab technicians, and other health care workers—fit right into the ministry of healing, as do visits by non-medical people to those who are ill or injured or challenged, plus prayer with them and for them. As we saw in the story of The Good Samaritan, Jesus encouraged us to become people who do or support these kinds of things (Lk 10:25–37).

Immediately before Jesus told the story of the Good Samaritan he told a listener that we should love our neighbors as we love ourselves. Apparently, the man to whom

Jesus spoke didn't want to waste his love on anyone who wasn't his neighbor, so he asked Jesus, "Who is our neighbor?" Jesus responded by telling "The Story of the Good Samaritan." That story is about a man who had been beaten severely, robbed, and left in dangerous circumstances on a road that ran between Jerusalem and Jericho. Several people saw him but passed by.

The good Samaritan went up to the man—which was a risky thing to do because the robbers who attacked the man might have been waiting to ambush anyone who tried to help the man. Indeed, the man lying on the road might have been one of the robbers pretending to be injured! But robbers did not attack, and the man was genuinely suffering, so the good Samaritan bandaged the man's wounds, put him on his donkey, took him to an inn, and told the innkeeper to take care of him. Then he told the innkeeper that he, the Samaritan, had to continue on his journey but that he would return to pay the innkeeper for whatever care the injured man needed.

Jesus ended this story by saying to his listeners, "Go and do likewise." The point of the story is that the good neighbor was the one who stopped and "showed mercy" to the man. Note: Jesus didn't answer the question that his interlocutor asked. Jesus was saying to the man that he had asked the wrong question. The question isn't, "Who are my neighbors?" so I can figure out whom to exclude from my compassion. The question is, "Am I a good neighbor?" Hence, by means of his story Jesus did not tell the man who his neighbors were; rather, he told the man to be a good neighbor—to be a compassionate person.

9. DIGNITY OF THE INDIVIDUAL

Jesus told his followers to treat people with dignity and compassion. Don't insult people. Don't call them fools. If you remember that someone has a legitimate complaint against you, don't ignore them as though they are not important. Make reconciliation your first priority. Even if you're in the temple worshipping, as we earlier heard Jesus say, break off what you are doing and go make amends to the person whom you have hurt or to whom you owe something (Mt 5:21-24).

Jesus emphasized treating one's *parents* with dignity when he criticized those who gave money to the Temple in place of helping their parents. Apparently there was a man-made rule that allowed Jews in his time to substitute helping the Temple for helping their parents, thereby allowing people to sidestep the commandment that we honor our father and mother. Jesus was critical of that rule.

We have also seen how Jesus treated lepers with dignity. Once when Jesus came down from a mountain and went into a nearby city, a man full of leprosy came to Jesus, knelt before him, and asked for help (Lk5:12; Mt 8:1-2). People in those days, understandably, were terrified by leprosy—which could horribly disfigure a person and even cause fingers and toes to deteriorate and fall off. Today we still hear the expression that someone was avoided "like he was a leper." What was Jesus' reaction to the leprous man who approached him? According to Mark 1.40-42, Jesus was "*Moved with pity*, stretched out his hand and *touched* him"! (my emphasis) Later in his gospel Mark tells us that in Bethany Jesus ate at the house of a leper named Simon (Mk 14:3). It is difficult for most of us to appreciate how compassionate and gutsy those actions of Jesus were. Perhaps the people today who can best appreciate what Jesus did are people with AIDS. They understand how demeaning and depressing it is to be shunned by others and how profoundly important being befriended and touched is to their sense of dignity and self-worth.

In another story Mark tells us that when Jesus came out of a mountain where he had gone to pray, he was met by a crowd. Out of the crowd came a father who knelt before Jesus and begged him to have mercy on his young son. His son apparently suffered from epileptic seizures that caused him to fall into fires and water, thereby injuring himself. Viewing epileptic seizures can be frightening to people who do not understand them, and especially to people who think they are caused by demons (as many people believed in Jesus' day). Jesus cured the boy, instead of shunning him, and he thereby treated both the boy and his father with dignity as well as compassion (Mk 9:14–29).

Jesus focused on character, not worldly success. For example, he pointed out to his disciples that a poor widow who put only two small coins into the treasury of the temple in Jerusalem had, from a spiritual point of view, put in more than some of those who had put in much more money. Why? Because the latter gave what they did not need whereas she gave money that she needed (Mk 12:41–44). By his comment Jesus affirmed the dignity of that indigent lady.

Shortly before his crucifixion, when a woman poured precious, fragrant oil over Jesus' head, the disciples criticized her for wasting a valuable resource. Jesus rebuked the disciples and elevated and affirmed the woman's dignity by saying that she had done "a beautiful thing" that would be told about all over the world (Mk 14:3-9). And indeed it has been. I just did it again!

Jesus also treated short people with dignity. Luke tells us that as Jesus was passing through Jericho, "A man was there named Zacchaeus; he was a chief tax collector and was rich. He was trying to see who Jesus was, but because of the crowd he could not, because he was short in stature. So he ran ahead and climbed a sycamore tree to see him, because he was going to pass that way. When Jesus came to the place, he looked up and said to him, 'Zacchaeus, hurry and come down; for I must stay at your house today.'" Luke adds that Zacchaeus hurried down "and was happy to welcome" Jesus. Perhaps Zacchaeus was what today is known as "a little person"—a little person whose dignity and worth Jesus affirmed (see Lk19:1-10).

Finally, I mention that Jesus treated effeminate men with dignity (Mk 14:12-16). Early on the day of the Last Supper, Jesus sent his disciples to prepare their Passover meal. The disciples asked where they should go to prepare the meal. Jesus told them to go into Jerusalem and they would be met by a man carrying a jar of water. That man would lead them to the room where they would have their Passover meal. The striking thing here is that carrying jars of water was usually a woman's job in that time, not a man's job, so the man they were to meet was in some way, for some reason, a womanly man. Yet Jesus had no problem sending the disciples to him, and Luke gives no indication that the disciples objected to meeting and following him. Rather, the man was treated with the dignity of being given a responsibility, being met with, and being followed.

10. JESUS WAS CRITICAL OF PREJUDICE

Jesus despised racism, ethnicism, and religionism. He set a clear example of trying to overcome racial, ethnic, and religious arrogance and hostility. As we have seen, in Jesus' time Samaritans and Jews were hostile to one another. They were intensely divided over a common heritage, somewhat like Roman Catholics and Protestants were during the Reformation. Yet on his final journey to Jerusalem, Jesus, who was a Jew, decided to stay in a Samaritan village—which was gracious and risky on his part. He sent some of his disciples ahead to make arrangements. The Samaritans said they did not want Jesus in their village. As Luke puts it, "On their way [the disciples] entered a village of the Samaritans to make ready for [Jesus]; but [the Samaritans] did not receive him, because his face was set toward Jerusalem" (Jews and Samaritans were divided over whether Jerusalem should be the center of worship for Israelites; Jews said yes; Samaritans said no, so the Samaritans did not want to host someone who was going to Jerusalem to worship.)

Luke says that when the Samaritans refused to welcome Jesus, his disciples James and John said, "'Lord, do you want us to command fire to come down from heaven and consume them?' But he turned and rebuked [them]. Then they went on to another village" (Lk9:51–56). Obviously, Jesus' disciples would have been happy to torch those bad ol' Samaritans and their village. But Jesus wouldn't permit it. And he didn't just say "No" to his disciples. He *rebuked* them for having such a desire.

On an earlier occasion when Jesus was traveling through Samaria, it was near noon and he was tired, so he stopped at a well. "A Samaritan woman," John tells us, "came to draw water, and Jesus said to her, 'Give me a drink.'" The woman was surprised that a Jew would even speak to her, much less ask her for water. "How is it," she said, "that you, a Jew, ask a drink of me, a woman of Samaria?" John adds this explanatory remark: "Jews do not share things in common with Samaritans." Jesus gentled and amazed the woman with his knowledge and openness. As a result she went into town and told other Samaritans about Jesus, so they asked him to stay with them, which he did for two days. By the time he left, we are told, many Samaritans had become his followers (Jn 4:1–9).

Then there is the story of the Good Samaritan (Lk10:33–35), which makes numerous points. Earlier we saw its emphasis on Jesus' compassion for the ill and the injured, and his desire that we each become a compassionate person. Another thing Jesus did by telling that story was to affirm the goodness of Samaritan people—thereby countering negative Jewish stereotypes of Samaritans. The story states that two Jews, traveling separately and at different times on an open highway, each saw but passed a robbed and wounded stranger without helping him. Perhaps they were in an urgent hurry; perhaps they were afraid the man was dead and they did not want to violate a Jewish law against contact with a corpse; perhaps they wanted to help but were concerned that the man might be a decoy who was working with bandits who would attack them if they stopped; perhaps they just didn't care about the man. Whatever their reasons, Jesus tells us that a Samaritan who came later did care, took the risks and accepted the expense and inconvenience of helping the man.

Along the same line, Luke says that when Jesus made his last trip to Jerusalem he passed through the region between Samaria and Galilee. "As he entered a village, ten lepers approached him. Keeping their distance, they called out, saying, 'Jesus, Master, have mercy on us!'" Luke says that Jesus didn't heal them immediately. Rather, he told them to go show themselves to the priests. On their way to see the priests, they were cleansed of their leprosy. Luke reports that only one of the ten turned back to thank Jesus. That exceptional man was a Samaritan (Lk17:11–19).

On yet another occasion Jesus went to the region of Tyre (which was outside of Israel in Phoenicia). "He entered a house and did not want anyone to know he was there. Yet he could not escape notice." A woman, whose little daughter had an affliction, came to Jesus, bowed down at his feet, and begged him to help her daughter. "Now the woman was a Gentile, of Syro-phoenician origin." Hence, the woman was neither a Jew nor a Samaritan. Jesus challenged her to see if she was prejudiced against Jews. He told her, in brief, that the Jewish people should be taken care of before Gentiles are taken care of. Moreover, he put his point in an insulting way, forcing the woman to confront any prejudice in her heart. Jesus told her, "Let the children be fed first, for it is not fair to take the children's food and throw it to the dogs."

By her response to Jesus' taunt, the woman showed profound humility and desperate love for her daughter. In one of the most moving stories I've ever read, the mother said, "Sir, even the dogs under the table eat the children's crumbs." Jesus was deeply moved and said to her, "For saying that, your daughter has been cured." In these ways Jesus challenged prejudice in others and reached out indiscriminately to Jews, Samaritans, and Gentiles (Mk 7:24–30).

But what about the Romans? In Jesus' time, Israel was a conquered, occupied, oppressed, exploited part of the Roman Empire. Many Jews hated the Romans, and especially the Roman soldiers. Nonetheless, when a Roman soldier appealed to Jesus to help a beloved servant who was paralyzed and in great distress, Jesus healed the man's servant (Mt 8:5–13).

In the Sermon on the Mount, Jesus said, "Love your enemies and pray for those who persecute you, so that you may be children of your Father in heaven; for he makes his sun rise on the evil and on the good, and sends rain on the righteous and the unrighteous. For," he continues, "if you love those who love you, what reward do you have? Do not even the tax collectors do the same? And if you greet only your brothers and sisters, what more are you doing than others? Do not even the Gentiles do the same? Be perfect, therefore, as your heavenly Father is perfect" (Mt 5:43–48).

In the stories presented in this section we have seen that Jesus lived his philosophy as well as preached it. He didn't turn away people who were Samaritans or Romans or Greeks, even though he was a Jew and the Jews were hated by many of those people, and even though many Jews considered those people to be enemies or heretical or unclean. I think we have to love and admire someone who treated all people with kindness and dignity.

11. HUMILITY

Jesus came from a lowly social background. His father was a laborer. His mother gave birth to him in a stable. He grew up in humble circumstances among working-class people, and though he could have used his extraordinary intelligence and energy to elevate his lot in life, he stayed among ordinary people because he loved them and wanted to help them.

Jesus was a humble person. He did not brag about himself or exalt himself above others. In addition to being humble himself, Jesus forbad his disciples to exalt themselves. He commanded them to be servants of others, not masters. People often think that to be great means to lord it over other people and exercise authority over them. By contrast, Jesus told his disciples, "It shall not be so among you; but whoever would be great among you must be your servant, and whoever would be first among you must be your slave; even as the Son of man came not to be served but to serve, and to give his life as a ransom for many" (Mt 20:26–28). It is interesting to note why Jesus made the preceding remark. He did so after the mother of two of his disciples started a quarrel among all the disciples. How did she do that? By asking Jesus to place her two sons on his immediate right and left in his kingdom!

On yet another occasion a dispute arose among the disciples as to which of them should be regarded as the greatest. Jesus said to them, "The kings of the Gentiles exercise lordship over them; and those in authority over them are called benefactors. But not so with you; rather let the greatest among you become as the youngest, and the leader as one who serves. For which is the greater, one who sits at table, or one who serves? Is it not the one who sits at table? But I am among you as one who serves" (Lk22:24–27).

According to John, after Jesus made the preceding statement (during the Last Supper) he made it clear that he was utterly serious by washing and drying the feet of the disciples. When Peter refused to allow Jesus to wash his feet—perhaps convinced that Jesus *wanted* the disciples to refuse to allow him to do such a humble thing and wanted them, instead, to exalt him as Lord—Jesus made it perfectly clear to Peter and the other disciples that he was serious that the paradigm for his followers was servant, not ruler; was benefactor, not beneficiary; was giver, not taker; was provider not exploiter. So Jesus told Peter that if Peter did not allow Jesus to wash his feet, then "you have no part in me." That caused Peter to relent. Then Jesus washed Peter's feet and said, "Do you know what I have done to you? You call me Teacher and Lord; and you are right, for so I am. If I then, your Lord and Teacher, have washed your feet, you also ought to wash one another's feet. For I have given you an example, that you also should do as I have done to you." "If you know these things," Jesus added, "blessed are you if you do them" (Jn 13:1–17). And so we have another reason for loving Jesus—because he directed his followers to serve one another rather than lord it over one another (and, of course, one can serve others by being a good manager as well as by being a good worker).

12. GENEROSITY

As we saw in the last section, Jesus emphasized service. He taught us by word and example to be altruistic not selfish, generous not stingy. We have seen also that he was trying to get his followers to become a certain kind of people, rather to than live by rules. But he was not above motivating good behavior by telling his followers that their actions had consequences for themselves. Along this line he said: "the measure you give will be the measure you get back." Therefore, instead of giving or selling someone a cup of flour that is fluffed up and a bit short, we should give "good measure, pressed down, shaken together, running over" (Lk 6:37–40). Also, "As you wish that men would do to you, do so to them" (Lk 6:31). This is "the Golden Rule." The Silver Rule says, "Do not do to others what you would not have them do to you." Obviously, the Golden Rule requires greater generosity than the Silver Rule.

To a wealthy young man who asked Jesus what he must do to inherit eternal life, Jesus began by quoting the "do not" commandments from Exodus, chapter 20: do not commit adultery; do not steal; do not bear false witness; etc. But Jesus ended by saying "love your neighbor as yourself." In other words, to refrain from harming people is not enough. More is required. Jesus taught us to transform the world by making friends out of strangers and allies out of enemies. He asked, "If you love those that love you, what credit is that to you?" (Lk6:32–36) To transform the world, we need to do more.

For a final look at Jesus' urging that we be generous, consider the following statements that he made to his followers, keeping in mind that by "fruit" he meant "good works." "My Father is glorified by this," he said, "that you bear much fruit, and so prove to be my disciples. As the Father has loved me, so have I loved you; abide in my love. If you keep my commandments, you will abide in my love, just as I have kept my Father's commandments and abide in his love. These things I have spoken to you, that my joy may be in you, and that your joy may be full. This is my commandment, that you love one another as I have loved you. Greater love has no man than this, that a man lay down his life for his friends. You are my friends if you do what I command you" (Jn 15:8–14). Part of the meaning of the next to last verse might also be captured by saying, "Greater generosity has no man than this, that a man devote his life to his friends."

13. MOTHERS AND FATHERS

Jesus loved his mother. The last act of his life—while he was nailed to a cross in great pain, suffocating, and very near death—was (1) to make sure that someone would take care of his mother, and (2) that after his death his mother would still have a son to care for. It was, I believe, a deep and touching insight on Jesus' part that after his death his mother would benefit greatly from still having a son to care for. St. John clarifies what I mean: "When Jesus saw his mother and the disciple whom he loved standing beside her [near the cross where he was hanging], he said to his mother, 'Woman, here is your son.' Then he said to the disciple, 'Here is your mother.' And from that hour," John tells us, "the disciple took her into his own home" (Jn 19:25–27). That disciple was probably St. John himself.

We do not know much about the father of Jesus. He was alive when Jesus was 12, but apparently was dead when Jesus began his ministry at about age 30. We do know, however, that Jesus had the highest regard for fatherhood. When his disciples asked him to teach them a special prayer, he began it by teaching them to think of God as their father in heaven. In Jesus' time that was an unusual way to think of God. It was more common to think of God in ways that made God seem remote, mysterious, and forbidding. Moreover, thinking of God as father was not a late development in Jesus' mind. Recall that when he was 12 and his parents had to track him down at the Temple in Jerusalem, he seemed puzzled that they did not know where he would be. "Did you not know," he asked them, "that I must be in my father's house?" That house was the Temple in Jerusalem, the center of Jewish worship of Yahweh. Hence, even at 12, while his earthly father was still alive, Jesus had a very high opinion of fathers and thought of God as his heavenly father (Lk2:49).

14. LOYALTY

Jesus believed in rock-hard loyalty among friends. In John 10:11–13 he says that he is the Good Shepherd who will not abandon his flock when wolves threaten to attack, and that he will not abandon his followers like a hired keeper might abandon orphans when a storm breaks out (Jn 14:18).

Later Jesus confronted Peter on the issue of loyalty. Soon after Jesus was arrested, Peter was suspected of being one of Jesus' supporters and was questioned as to his connection to Jesus. Peter denied even knowing Jesus. After his resurrection, Jesus said to Peter, in so many words, "Peter, when I was arrested by the Romans, you ran from me like a false shepherd runs from wolves, or like an uncaring caretaker of orphans might abandon them in a storm. Yet you say you love me. Do you love me, Peter? If you do, then feed my sheep. Don't run from them when circumstances get difficult or dangerous" (John 21:15–17). Jesus didn't abandon *his* followers when the going got tough. He accepted stress, fatigue, danger, rejection, abuse, torment, and death for their sake. He showed ultimate loyalty to his followers. To paraphrase what he says in John 15:13, "Greater loyalty has no man than this, that a man lay down his life for his friends." And he did. And he deserves our love for that.

15. EMOTIONS

Some have reasoned that because God is perfect in all ways, therefore God is perfectly and unwaveringly blissful. Consequently, they have concluded that God is not made happier by our joys nor disturbed by our sorrows. Whether that argument is correct or not, whether God on high is emotionally affected by our joys and sorrows or not, Jesus certainly was. His emotional life was like ours. He felt joy, sorrow, anger, pain, tenderness, and temptation. The shortest sentence in the New Testament says, "Jesus wept" (Jn 11:35). He talked about how a shepherd rejoiced when he found his lost sheep, and how a poor old lady rejoiced when she found a coin she had lost. He understood those emotions. He felt them.

When a leper asked Jesus for help, we are told that Jesus was "moved by pity" (Mk 1:41). On another occasion when he saw a crowd of people, we are told that "he had compassion for them, because they were harassed and helpless, like sheep without a shepherd" (Mt 9:36). People knew Jesus was compassionate, so they appealed to his pity when they wanted help from him. When Lazarus was seriously ill, what did his sisters, Mary and Martha, do? They sent the following message to Jesus: "Lord, he whom you love is ill" (Jn 11:3). They were appealing to Jesus' affection and pity.

At that time Lazarus, Mary, and Martha were living in Bethany, where Jewish leaders had recently attempted to stone Jesus, so the disciples urged him not to go back there to help Lazarus. But Jesus loved Martha, Mary, and Lazarus so much that he went anyway; he went into danger so serious that his disciple Thomas said to the other disciples, "Let us also go, that we may die with him." Lazarus died several days before Jesus arrived. When he was met by Martha and Mary, who were deep in grief over their brother Lazarus's death, we are told that Jesus was deeply affected: "When Jesus saw [Mary] weeping, and the Jews who came with her weeping, he was deeply moved in spirit and troubled" and *he* began to weep. Then they went to Lazarus' tomb where Jesus was "deeply moved again" (Jn 11:33–38).

Another sign that Jesus was lovable because his emotions were like ours is that he often sighed deeply at the callousness and stubbornness of people who were hostile to him. As we saw earlier, he was especially grieved over the hard-heartedness of Jerusalem. "O Jerusalem, Jerusalem," he said, "killing the prophets and stoning those who are sent to you! How often would I have gathered your children together as a hen gathers her brood under her wings, and you would not!" (Mt 23:37) Luke tells us that when Jesus made his last trip to Jerusalem and looked down at the city, "he wept over it," in sorrow for its rejection of the things that make for peace, and in sadness for the things he knew it would suffer (Lk 19:41–44).

In the Garden of Gethsemane, shortly before he was arrested, as Jesus thought about his approaching fate "he began to be sorrowful and troubled. Then he said to [his disciples], 'My soul is very sorrowful, even to death; remain here, and watch with me.' And going a little farther, he fell on his face and prayed, 'My Father, if it be possible, let this cup pass from me; nevertheless, not as I will, but as thou wilt'" (Mt 26:36–39). Luke adds, "And being in agony he prayed more earnestly; and his sweat became like great drops of blood falling down upon the ground" (Lk 22:44). There can be no doubt that Jesus was not aloof like an Olympian god whom we can admire but not love. Jesus was one of us.

16. TEMPTATION

Jesus knew temptation. He understood this important, powerful element of human life. Recall that after he was baptized by his cousin John the Baptist, Jesus went into the wilderness by himself for a long time. Note: he did not go into the wilderness surrounded by friends. He went by himself. Moreover, as Mark puts it, "he was with the wild beasts"; he was not in a comfortable lodge with a full 'fridge and a courtesy bar. He fasted in the wilderness for a long time, became very hungry, and was tempted by the devil from every angle. (For a review of the devil's temptations of Jesus, refer back to section 2, "Mentally Tough," in Chapter 1).

Because of such experiences Jesus knew the power of temptation so intimately that he taught us to distinguish between meaning to do something and actually doing it. When his disciples were very sleepy but he needed them to stay awake in the Garden of Gethsemane, he told them, "Stay awake, and pray that you may not come into the time of temptation; the spirit indeed is willing, but the flesh is weak" (Mt 26:41). Moreover, when his disciples asked him to teach them a special prayer, he taught them to ask God, "lead us not into temptation." It is significant that Jesus devoted part of this very short prayer to the topic of temptation; he did so because he knew how *powerful* temptation is and how *destructive* it can be (Mt 6:13; Lk 11:4). He also sternly discouraged us from being the instruments by which others are tempted to sin. For example, using the expression "stumbling block" as a metaphor for a temptation to sin, he says in Mt 18:7, "Occasions for stumbling are bound to come, but woe to the one by whom the stumbling block comes!" Jesus is worthy of our love because he cared enough about us to condemn the temptations and behaviors that damage and destroy our lives.

17. HOPE

We love people who give us hope. Without hope, we despair. We give up. We resign ourselves to unhappiness. Sometimes, of course, we *should* give up hope. Sometimes loss of hope is a blessing. But those things are not true of the hope that Jesus gave us. Jesus gave us hope that evil and indifference, failure and loss, will not have the last word in history or in our lives. In the Sermon on Mount he gave encouragement to those who are humble, who mourn, who hunger and thirst for justice, who are persecuted for the sake of justice, who are merciful, who are pure in heart, who are peacemakers (Mt 5:1–12). For these things we should always hope.

On a later occasion Jesus placed a child by his side and said, "Whoever receives this child in my name receives me; and whoever receives me receives him who sent me" (Lk9:46–48). When he spoke those words he taught us that love is not just a subjective, earthly thing. Rather, love arises from the deepest depths of reality and rises to its highest heights; or to reverse the direction, love descends from the highest height of reality and goes down to its lowest depth. Love is rooted in God, who is the ground of all being; love arises from God, the source of all good things; love returns to God, in whom all good things find their fulfillment. Jesus taught us that we should never cease to hope that these things are true.

When Jesus said that the Kingdom of God is like a tiny mustard seed, and that it is like the small amount of leaven which is put into a large bowl of ingredients for making a loaf of bread, he was giving us hope (Lk13:18–21). Without the leaven you get something flat, hard, and tasteless; with the leaven you get a plump, soft loaf that is fragrant and tasty. Moreover, the tiny mustard seed grows into a shrub so large that birds can have a party in it—flitting, singing, and nesting.

By those analogies Jesus was saying, among other things, that a good deed is something that has good consequences, and those good consequences have more good consequences. Maybe in a northern environment Jesus would have said that the Kingdom of God is like a tiny snowball that starts rolling downhill, picking up more and more snowflakes, getting bigger and bigger until it is huge. Those analogies should give us hope, but we, like Jesus, have to take the initiative and the risks to get the ball rolling and keep it rolling, gathering speed and building size.

Jesus also said that God is like the father of the prodigal son. The prodigal son asked for his share of the inheritance that his father planned to give him. His father could have said "no" and made his son wait until his father's death to receive his inheritance, but instead the father gave his son his inheritance and his freedom. The son left, spent his money entertaining himself and his friends, and then was plunged into poverty. Eventually he came to his senses, repented, swallowed his pride, and humbly returned to his father. When his father saw him returning, he didn't reject his wayward son or punish him or humiliate him. Rather, while his son was visible but still some distance from the family farm, "his father saw him and had compassion, and ran and embraced him and kissed him" (Lk 15:20). Jesus said that is how God feels about *us*, and surely that should give us hope that whatever we have done that we ought not to have done, and whatever we ought to have done that we have not done, if we turn around and turn back to God, God will welcome us. I certainly hope so.

18. STRESS AND PEACE

Jesus understood stress. He was under a great deal of it. He also understood the stress that we are under and he tried to help us cope with it. Consider some of the memorable statements he made on this topic. "Come to me, all you that are weary and are carrying heavy burdens, and I will give you rest. Take my yoke upon you, and learn from me; for I am gentle and humble in heart, and you will find rest for your souls. For my yoke is easy, and my burden is light" (Mt 11:28–30). Also, Jesus assured his followers that he was not going to leave them to struggle on their own after his death. He told them, "Peace I leave with you; my peace I give to you; not as the world gives do I give to you. Let not your hearts be troubled; neither let them be afraid" (Jn 14:27).

There are more such statements that Jesus made during his life, but let's skip over them and look at those made by Jesus after his death and resurrection. After Jesus' death some women went to his tomb to mourn him. When they did not find him they were stunned and worried, but an angel appeared to them and said, "Do not be afraid" (Mk 16:6). (That is also what an angel told the shepherds who were terrified by the angel's announcement that a savior had been born, Lk2:8–11.)

Finally, note that the first two times that Jesus appeared to the disciples after his resurrection he began by saying to them, "*Peace* be with you" (John 20:19–29; my emphasis). In spite of what Jesus said, the disciples "were startled and frightened, and supposed that they saw a spirit." Jesus calmed them by saying, "Why are you troubled, and why do questionings rise in your hearts?" Then he asked them for something to eat (fish). That was a clever move on Jesus' part. The last thing they all did together *before* Jesus' death was share a meal ("the Last Supper"). The first thing Jesus did when they were all together *after* his death was eat some of their food! Few things are more stress relieving than sharing food with friends. And, of course, eating fish assured the disciples that Jesus was real and not a ghost or an apparition (Lk24:36–3).

19. WORK

We should love Jesus because he gave dignity to work and the world of work. He was a carpenter; several of his close friends were fishermen; he ate with or helped housewives, tax collectors, soldiers, administrators, and scholars. He told stories about shepherds and farmers. He knew the work world; he was part of the work world; he loved working people.

20. MERCY

By word and example Jesus taught us to be merciful to others, and he taught others to be merciful to us (thank you, Jesus!). Sometimes Jesus appealed to an ideal to motivate us to be merciful. He said, for example, "Be merciful, just as your Father [in heaven] is merciful" (Lk 6:36). But he also understood that sometimes we need to be motivated by selfish considerations, so if we can't be merciful out of compassion, we should consider the personal consequences of not being merciful: "With the judgment you pronounce," he said, "you will be judged" (Mt 7:2). That certainly gives *me* pause. He also said, "Do not judge, and you will not be judged; do not condemn, and you will not be condemned. Forgive, and you will be forgiven; give, and it will be given to you" (Lk 6:36–38). Most famous on this topic is what he taught us in the Lord's Prayer: "Forgive us our debts *as we forgive* our debtors" and "Forgive us our trespasses *as we forgive* those who trespass against us" (Mt 6:9–15; Lk 11:1–4). Such an attitude is so much better than an attitude of hardness or vengeance. It is rooted in humble recognition that we are all sinners who need mercy. It is also rooted in the knowledge that being merciful to a person can profoundly touch and change that person. Grim condemnation never does.

21. SYMPATHY

Jesus was a sympathetic person. As we saw earlier, he greeted and touched people with frightening diseases and personalities. He told crowds of weary, anxious people, "Come to me, all who labor and are heavy laden, and I will give you rest" (Mt 11:28–30). When Jesus saw the only son of a widow being carried in a funeral procession and the mother crying, "he had compassion for her and said to her, 'Do not weep.'" Then he restored the son to life and "gave him to his mother" (Lk7:11–17). What a touching scene that must have been. Then there was Jairus, the ruler of a synagogue, whose daughter was dying. In a heartrending scene Jairus literally fell at Jesus' feet and begged him repeatedly to make his daughter well, so Jesus followed Jairus to his house and did just that (Mk 5:21–43).

When Jesus heard about the execution of his cousin John the Baptist, he withdrew by boat so he could be alone. While he was gone, a crowd gathered on shore where they expected him to return. When he returned, surely he was still grieved by the brutal murder of John and riveted by the pivotal significance that John's death had for what he must do next, yet we are told, "As he went ashore he saw a great throng, and he had compassion on them, and healed their sick." Who could have faulted him if instead he had told the crowd he was too sad, too tired, too stressed-out to help them that day. But he didn't, and when the disciples finally urged Jesus to send the crowd away so they could find something to eat, Jesus said, "They need not go away; you give them something to eat."

As we saw earlier, the disciples tried to wriggle out of that by saying they had only five loaves of bread and two fish, which wouldn't even begin to feed such a crowd. But Jesus insisted they share their food with the crowd. Then something marvelous happened. Maybe the disciples knew the crowd would have brought food, and they were just trying to get rid of the crowd by telling Jesus that they should be sent away to find food. Maybe the disciples didn't realize the crowd had food, but Jesus realized it. Maybe it was a miracle (Matthew 14:13–21). Whatever happened, enough food appeared for everyone to eat comfortably. Matthew says that after the crowd ate, Jesus sent the disciples away while he dismissed the crowd *by himself*—as though out of love he wanted to be alone with the crowd—without the static so often caused by the disciples, who often "just didn't get it." (See a second story about feeding a crowd in Mk 8:1–10.)

Here is a final example of Jesus' deep sympathy. As he was going into Jerusalem two blind men standing along the road cried out, "Have mercy on us, Son of David!" But "The crowd rebuked them, telling them to be silent." So what did Jesus do? "Jesus stopped and called them, saying, 'What do you want me to do for you?' They said to him, 'Lord, let our eyes be opened.' And Jesus in pity touched their eyes" (Mt 20:29–34). My God, what sympathy! How can we help but love such a man?

22. GOOD NEWS

We love good news and those who bring it. One of the most beloved passages in the Bible says, "How beautiful upon the mountains are the feet of the messenger who announces peace, who brings good news, who announces salvation" (Isaiah 52:7). Jesus brought us the best possible news. He assured us that God exists and is good, wise, and powerful. An example of how profoundly that belief can calm us comes from a time when Jesus and his disciples were crossing the Sea of Galilee. A fierce squall came up quickly and engulfed them. The disciples were terrified, but Jesus was not. In fact, he remained asleep while waves were swamping the boat! When the disciples woke Jesus, "He rebuked the winds and the sea; and there was a great calm" (Mt 8:23–27). The calm of the sea mirrored the calm in his heart, and he tries to convey that deep calm to us by assuring us that no matter how bleak things might seem, ultimately a good, wise, and powerful God is in control of all things (Mk 4:35–41).

23. PRIORITIES

Sometimes we don't know what our priorities should be, and sometimes when we do know what our priorities should be, forgetfulness or emotion causes us to get our priorities out of order. Jesus understood this. He also understood how destructive it is when we don't put first things first, second things second, and so on. Hence, many of his sayings are intended to get us to think about our priorities, to set them right, and to stick to them. For example, he said, "Take heed, and beware of all covetousness; for a man's life does not consist in the abundance of his possessions" (Lk12:15). Also, "Do not be anxious about your life, what you shall eat or what you shall drink, nor about your body, what you shall put on. Is not life more than food, and the body more than clothing?" (Mt 6:25) "Seek first [God's] kingdom and his righteousness and all these things shall be yours as well" (Lk12:33).

Sometimes what Jesus said is scary and seems wrong. For example, he said, "He who loves father or mother more than me is not worthy of me; and he who loves son or daughter more than me is not worthy of me" (Mt 10:37). That might seem wrong, but think about what Jesus stood for. Think about the Kingdom of God that he exalted and promoted throughout his ministry. Jesus and the kingdom stand for brotherhood and sisterhood against racism, for sincerity against hypocrisy, for compassion against callousness. I think Jesus' point is that, for example, if a person is willing to tolerate or abet racism rather than disagree with a racist father or mother, or if a person is willing to be hypocritical or callous toward someone in order to maintain the affection of a son or daughter, then that person is putting less important things ahead of the Kingdom of God and is not ready for residence therein.

24. LOVE

Jesus' life and teachings exalt love and condemn hate, insensitivity, and indifference. In John 13:34–35 he says, "A new commandment I give to you, that you love one another; even as I have loved you, that you also love one another. By this all men will know that you are my disciples, if you have love for one another." Moments later he says, "He who has my commandments and keeps them, he it is who loves me; and he who loves me will be loved by my Father, and I will love him and manifest myself to him" (Jn 14:21). In the first part of the preceding verse, Jesus is saying: "The one who loves me is the one who obeys me." How do we obey him? By following his new commandment that we love one another as he loved us. But note: love of Jesus is not merely an ethical philosophy. It does not consist of conformity to a moral code. It consists of conforming to the will of someone we love. It consists of pursuing the ideal of becoming a loving person, as that ideal was taught by Jesus and exemplified in his life.

The preceding quotations all come from the Gospel of John, but they are quite consistent with statements in the other Gospels. For example, in the Gospel According to Mark, when a lawyer asked Jesus which commandment is most important, Jesus gave him two commandments for the price of one. "The first," he said, "is, 'Hear, O Israel, the Lord our God, the Lord is one; and you shall love the Lord your God with all your heart, and with all your soul, and with all your mind, and with all your strength.' The second," he said, "is this, 'You shall love your neighbor as yourself.' There is no commandment greater than these" (Mk 12:28–34).

In the Gospel According to Matthew Jesus adds, "On these two commandments hang all the law and the prophets" (Mt 22:34–40). Implications of those two commandments are set out in Matthew 25, the grand finale of Jesus' teaching before he set out on his fateful trip to Jerusalem. There, in Matthew 25, he tells us that the Kingdom of God has been prepared "from the foundation of the world" for those who feed the hungry, give drink to the thirsty, welcome strangers, clothe the naked, take care of the sick, and visit those in prison—which is tantamount to saying that the Kingdom of God has been prepared for and awaits those who perform acts of love. How can we help but love someone who taught and embodied such love?

25. GOD WITH US

When Jesus was born, his father Joseph was told in a dream that he should name Jesus "Immanuel," which literally means "God with us." There are different theories as to what it means to say that God was with us in Jesus. Classic meanings of this belief can be found in I John 4:7–12 and 2 Corinthians 5:16–21. In some sense all Christians believe that God was with us in Jesus. If you believe that God is love, it is easy to believe that in Jesus God was with us (I Jn 4:16; see also Romans 8:38–39). It was out of love that Jesus promised he would not leave us alone. He promised that after his death God would still be with us. "If you love me," he said, "you will keep my commandments. And I will pray the Father, and he will give you another Counselor, to be with you forever, even the Spirit of truth" (Jn 14:15–16). Some lovers of Jesus never have an earth shaking religious experience, but all of them, I believe, have a warm sense of Jesus' love and presence. And that is another reason to love Jesus: he cared enough about us to provide for us even after his departure from this earth.

Part II

Lovers of Jesus

3

What Makes a Christian?

WHEN WE LOOK AT the history of Christianity we discover many forms of faith and practice. Diverse versions of the church emerged quite early as sincere people tried to figure out what is essential to being a Christian. Some of those versions of Christianity have not survived. Many have—and new ones continue to emerge. In our consumerist society the denominations that have survived are sometimes thought of as a smorgasbord for people to choose among. Thinking that way, however, would trivialize what those denominations stand for. Choosing a denomination is a serious thing. It is not like choosing food at a smorgasbord. I prefer to think of the multiplicity of denominations as a spectrum that contains many possible ways of being Christian. Which of those denominations one chooses should represent serious thought on the part of the chooser. It should not simply represent what one enjoys most, as at a holiday smorgasbord.

At a smorgasbord the factor that most often determines our choices is simply what tastes best. However, another factor should determine our choices even at a smorgasbord. Namely, which choices will promote and maintain our health, even if those choices will not please our palates as much as some other choices. Fortunately, some foods that are good for us also taste good! Similarly, some religions that "taste good" to us are good for us. Religion can give us some of the most profound pleasures of life, and the pleasures that a religion gives are important. Examples of such pleasures are a feeling of the presence of the divine, spiritual fellowship with and support from other people, hope, consolation, and a feeling of strength in the face of adversity. Even more important, though—as with food—is how healthy a religion is for us. Does it promote self-respect? Does it promote respect for others? Does it promote fairness? justice? humility? friendship? compassion? peace? cooperation? excellence?

In addition to pleasure and health there is a third factor that comes into play with the choice of a religion. It goes beyond considerations of pleasure and health and does not apply to food choices. This third factor is *truth*. A tomato is not true or false. It just is a tomato. Of course it may be an excellent tomato or a rotten tomato, a red tomato or a green tomato, but it's still a tomato. A fake tomato is not a tomato. It only appears to be a tomato. If I *believe* that an object is a tomato, then my belief is either true or false. But the object just is whatever it is. It is, then, *beliefs* that are true or false, so when we choose a religion, we must decide whether the beliefs of that religion are true or false. That accounts in large part for why there are so many different religions and so many different versions of each religion. Good, sincere, intelligent people can differ as to whether a certain belief is true or is false.

Some people are alienated from Christianity because there are so many denominations that disagree with one another. Denominations disagree not just on minor issues but also on fundamental issues, such as baptism, the Lord's Supper, the Trinity, and how the church should be organized. These people think that if any denomination were the true version of Christianity, it would be *obvious* that it was true, and there would not be so much disagreement. But there is a lot of disagreement; therefore, they say, because no denomination is *obviously* true, therefore no denomination is true.

Some other folks are alienated from Christianity—but not because denominations differ from one another. These folks hold that disagreement among humans is inevitable, but, they say, that doesn't mean no one is right. Scientists sometimes disagree with one another, but that doesn't mean that none of them is right. The problem these people have is that they can't find a denomination they think is true. They like one denomination a lot, but they can't go along with some of its practices. They like another denomination a lot, but they can't accept all of its beliefs. So they work their way through all the denominations of which they are aware, yet they cannot agree enough with any of them to join.

An important thing to realize about many of these discontented people is that even though they cannot in good conscience join a denomination, they love Jesus. They are deeply moved by his life and his death. They are touched by his teachings and the stories about him in the New Testament. They are moved by hymns about Jesus, and love to sing or hear them. Many of these people pray to Jesus and strive to live by his teachings. Some feel his presence. Some attend a church regularly but do not join it. As a result they are saddened and confused that they cannot find a place in Christianity where they can join with other people in devotion to Jesus.

These are people who really do love Jesus and would like to belong to a church, but cannot do so for a reason mentioned above or for some other honorable reason. Because they do not belong to a church, they think they are not Christians; or because they do not belong to a church, they think it would be hypocritical for them to think of themselves as Christians or to identify themselves as Christians. But I think that what makes a person a Christian is simply profound love of Jesus. It was that kind of love that gave birth to the church and gave it strength to survive in hostile circumstances. As the great Jewish historian Josephus (37–100 AD) observed, the church thrived because "those who had in the first place come to love him did not give up their affection for him" (Josephus, *Jewish Antiquities* 18:63–64). That still explains why Christianity is here.

If I am right, then I want to tell doubters who love Jesus that they can think of themselves as Christians and can identify themselves as Christians even if they do not yet feel comfortable joining a denomination. In the next chapter we will explore what a denomination is, how denominations might think of themselves in relation to one another, and how they might make themselves available to the people mentioned above.

4

Denominations and Love of Jesus

THE WORD "RELIGION" COMES from the Latin word "religare," which means to bind or join things together (a "*lig*ament" binds one bone to another). The Buddhist religion consists of people who are bound together by their devotion to Buddha. Christianity consists of people who are bound together by their devotion to Jesus. A denomination is a distinct group of people *within* a religion—distinct because its members have a belief or practice that other groups in their religion do not have. For example, Reform Jews are permitted to eat pork but Orthodox Jews are not. Within Christianity there are many denominations, some as similar as peaches and plums; some as different as bananas and broccoli.

The name of a denomination often expresses one of its special beliefs or practices. Sometimes the name expresses one of the denomination's central convictions (1) about what one must believe about God or Jesus in order to be correct, or (2) about how the Church should be organized, or (3) about how the sacraments should be understood and conducted. (But of course the name of a denomination never conveys everything about its beliefs and practices, and there is usually more than one belief or practice that distinguishes one denomination from another.)

Consider the following examples of denominational names. "Baptists" are distinguished in part by their beliefs about baptism. All Christian denominations I know of practice baptism, but Baptists believe that only people who are mature enough to understand what baptism is should be baptized; hence, they believe in "adult baptism" or "believers baptism" but not in "infant baptism." Baptists also believe baptism should be by full immersion of the body in water and not by mere sprinkling or pouring of water on the head. Many other denominations, however, believe that the sooner a person is baptized, the better. So they baptize infants, as well as children and adults, and they usually perform baptism by sprinkling or pouring a small amount of water on the head rather than by full immersion of the body.

On the topic of church organization and governance, Episcopalians believe in an episcopal form of church governance. "Episcopus" is a Greek word that means "bishop." Episcopalians believe that in addition to individual priests or ministers who preside over individual churches, there should also be bishops. Bishops are ministers who exercise leadership over groups of individual churches and who have derived their authority from an unbroken series of bishops going back to Saint Peter and the apostles, who received their authority directly from Jesus.

Roman Catholics, like Episcopalians, believe in bishops and the historical transmission of authority from Jesus to the present by "the laying on of hands." Each new bishop can be and is created only by the approval of those who are already bishops. They signify their approval by placing their hands on the person who is to become a new bishop. Roman Catholics also believe that Jesus gave supreme earthly authority over the entire church to St. Peter, the first bishop of Rome, and to his successors. Indeed, in the name "Roman Catholic" the word "Catholic" means "universal." Hence, Roman Catholics believe that the Bishop of Rome (the Pope) has ultimate earthly authority over the entire Church on earth, including other bishops.

By contrast, Episcopalians do not believe in the ultimate authority of the bishop of Rome (the Pope), and "Congregationalists" do not believe that any individual or external group of humans should have authority over the local congregation, so they do not believe in bishops at all. They believe that the local congregation has the right and authority to make and live by its own decisions—under the guidance of the Bible and the Holy Spirit. Many more examples could be given, but the preceding examples should be sufficient to show how instructive the name of a denomination can be.

Now if you love Jesus and have a strong conviction about how or when baptism should be done, then of course you should join the Baptists, the Catholics, or whichever group most fully shares your conviction. The same point applies to convictions about church authority, or what happens to the bread and wine used in the Lord's Supper, etc. But what if you are *attracted* to a denomination yet are not comfortable enough with its beliefs or practices to join? As I write this paragraph, it is the Christmas season, so here is one of my Christmas wishes: that every denomination will create an "affiliate" category for people who love Christ and are attracted to their church, but, because of some doctrine or practice (or because they feel unworthy), are not yet comfortable enough to join—and may never be. Such a category would allow people to declare their love of Christ and identify themselves as Christians to the church and the world, plus it would draw them into active fellowship with a church and identify them so that the priest or minister of the congregation could engage them in appropriate discussions and activities.

While I am Christmas wishing I would like to add that I would be delighted if all denominations identified themselves *primarily* as "Lovers of Jesus" and *secondarily* as something else. Remember: what makes a person a Christian is profound love of Jesus and devotion to him. Every sincere Christian is a lover of Christ Jesus, and there are many sincere Christians who are Amish, Baptist, Catholic, Disciples, Episcopalian, Lutheran, Mennonite, Methodist, Orthodox, Pentecostal, Presbyterian, Reformed, and more. So I will be happy if all denominations begin calling themselves "Lovers of Jesus" and then add a subtitle to emphasize a doctrine or practice that distinguishes them from others. For example, "Lovers of Jesus: Baptist," "Lovers of Jesus: Holiness," "Lovers of Jesus: Lutheran," "Lovers of Jesus: Roman Catholic," "Lovers of Jesus: Greek Orthodox," "Lovers of Jesus: Pentecostal," "Lovers of Jesus: Unitarian," and so on.

Among Christian denominations there is a wide ranging *number* of beliefs and practices that one must accept in order to become a member. Perhaps the greatest number of beliefs and practices that one must accept to become a member is in the Roman Catholic and Eastern Orthodox Churches. Perhaps the fewest beliefs and practices that one must accept are in the United Church of Christ and the Disciples of Christ. If, however, you cannot in good conscience join any established denomination as a full member or affiliate (if that option is available), and if you believe that a personal declaration that you want to know and live the love of Jesus should be sufficient for church membership, then maybe it's time to start a new denomination.

You might be thinking that the last thing the world needs is one more Christian denomination. We already have so many! Indeed, it may be that all lovers of Jesus can be accommodated by denominations that already exist. That would certainly make life simpler, and I urge non-member lovers of Jesus to examine established denominations carefully before proceeding independently. But perhaps there is need and room for at least one more denomination. This denomination would require for membership only that a person confess their love for Jesus, their desire to "know him more clearly and follow him more nearly," and their desire to join with others who have already declared their love for Jesus.

As in previous cases, the name of this denomination, as I envision it, would capture what is most important to it, namely, knowing and living the love of Jesus in community with others who want to do the same. Hence, it will be distinguished from other denominations not by a subtitle but by the absence of a subtitle. It's name will simply be "Lovers of Jesus."

Members of "Lovers of Jesus" will be drawn together and held together by their love of Jesus. They will be united by love of a person rather than by convictions about a doctrine or practice. They will gather together to testify to their love of Christ, to help one another learn more about Christ, to praise him, to come to know him more personally, to share their love of Christ with one another, and to allow his love to flow into them and through them—*into them* for uplift, solace, strength, and guidance; *through them* to those who are hurting from physical or emotional problems: disability, injury, illness, trauma, addiction, deprivation, loneliness, depression, oppression, exploitation, meaninglessness, etc.

In brief, Lovers of Jesus, as a group or denomination, will simply join around love for Jesus. Its members will be united by love of a person, not by commitment to a doctrine or ritual. Of course other denominations also are united by love of Jesus! But they are united by love of Jesus plus a special doctrine or practice. I am just trying to make a place for those who love Jesus but are not ready to subscribe to all the doctrines or practices of the denominations with which they are familiar.

To summarize, if you have strong convictions about particular doctrines or practices, such as the proper way to baptize or how the church should be organized or whether there should be a single head of the Church universal, then you should join a church that holds to the doctrine or practice that you believe is so important. But if you do not have any such strong conviction, yet you love Jesus, what he did and what he stood for, then I hope you will identify yourself as "a lover of Jesus" and "affiliate" with some local church or start a group of "Lovers of Jesus."

To put these points a bit differently, if you are profoundly moved by the love of Jesus, if you want to live in that love and know it better, if you want to experience the love of Jesus, if you want to let the love that comes to you from Jesus flow through you to others, then you are a Christian and should not hesitate to identify yourself as such, and you should join or at least affiliate with some denomination, or start a group of Lovers of Jesus. At the very least, Lovers of Jesus, as a group or denomination, would be a gathering place for unaffiliated lovers of Jesus until they can "graduate" to one of the established denominations by virtue of coming to believe there are specific doctrines or practices that a church should observe. And if they never "graduate," they will still have lived a life rich in fellowship with Christ and others devoted to Him.

5

Reasons to Doubt Jesus

As we saw at the end of chapter 1, Jesus encouraged us to use our minds, and he engaged us in doing so by telling parables that provoke thought rather than providing easy answers. People who dislike religion or do not understand it dismiss it sometimes because, they say, they don't believe in "blind faith." Jesus didn't, either—as I will illustrate in the next chapter. In this chapter what I want to do is point out that even people who love Jesus have had problems with some of the things he said or did, and I want to show that when people who loved Jesus raised such issues or had such problems, he did not reject them. He embraced them. For that reason, lovers of Jesus should embrace people who love Jesus but have a problem with something he said or did. Now let's look at some of those problems, and in the next chapter I will show that Jesus accepted and embraced people who had doubts about him or objections to him. (Keep in mind that I am not saying that all of the following difficulties are true or justified. I am simply reporting nine reasons why people have had difficulty believing in Jesus or might have difficult believing in him. My list is, of course, not exhaustive.)

1. PREDESTINATION

Some people are disturbed by the idea that Jesus believed that from eternity God determined who would be saved and who would be damned, so that whether we are saved or damned has absolutely nothing t
o do with our choices. According to the most stringent doctrine of predestination, God decided before creation *everything* that happens in history—including whether we believe in Jesus or not.

Whether Jesus believed this is controversial, but here are a few statements by Jesus that have led some Christians to believe in predestination. John 6:44: "No one can come to me unless drawn by the Father who sent me." John 15:16: "You did not choose me but I chose you." In John 17:6, speaking to God, Jesus says, "I have made your name known to those whom you gave me from the world. They were yours, and you gave them to me." A few verses later, still speaking to God, Jesus says of his followers, "I protected in your name them that you have given me. I guarded them, and not one of them was lost except the one destined to be lost." Presumably, "the one destined to be lost" from among Jesus' followers was Judas Iscariot, who betrayed Jesus to Jewish authorities; the other disciples were destined to be saved. It appears that none of them had a choice as to whether he would be saved or lost. Their fates were predestined.

There is more. According to John 10:24–30, some people asked Jesus, "If you are the Messiah, tell us plainly." Jesus replied, "I have told you, and you do not believe . . . because you do not belong to my sheep. My sheep hear my voice. I know them, and they follow me." In other words,

Jesus' questioners had *not* been chosen by God to believe in Jesus, so they did not believe in him. Of his believers, Jesus goes on to say, "No one will snatch them out of my hand. What my Father has given me is greater than all else, and no one can snatch it out of the Father's hand." In Mark 13:19-20 Jesus says that when history as we know it comes to an end, there will be such suffering that if those days were not cut short, "no one would be saved"; however, he adds, "*for the sake of the elect*, whom he [the Father] chose, he has cut short those days" (my emphasis).

Some people are critical of presdestinationism because to them it doesn't seem fair or just or loving to damn people who had no choice in the matter, and since God wouldn't do anything unfair, unjust, or unloving, those people don't believe God predestines anyone to damnation. Hence, those people think that if Jesus believed in predestination, he was mistaken in doing so. (By contrast to the preceding, there are many Christians in the Calvinist and Reformed traditions who adhere to and defend the doctrine of predestination.)

2. ASK AND IT WILL BE GIVEN

Here is another difficulty that some people have. Once upon a time Jesus was hungry, saw a fig tree, and went to get figs from it, but the tree had none, so Jesus cursed it, and it immediately withered. Tree lovers may think it mean-spirited that Jesus destroyed a fig tree for not having figs—especially when, according to St. Mark, it was not yet the season for figs! [There is an interesting discrepancy between Mark's fig tree story (11:12-24) and Matthew's (21:17-22). In Matthew's story the tree withered immediately. In Mark's story it seems that the tree did not wither immediately. Perhaps the stories are of different trees, but they seem to be of the same tree.] Some people also have difficulty with the idea that Jesus had the power to wither a tree on command. And if he did have that kind of power, why didn't he just command the tree to produce figs instead of destroying it?

An even more serious difficulty arises from what Jesus said when the disciples asked him, regarding the withering of the fig tree, "How did you do that?" Matthew says that Jesus answered, "Truly, I say to you, if you have faith and never doubt, you will not only do what has been done to this fig tree, but even if you say to this mountain, 'Be taken up and cast into the sea,' it will be done. And whatever you ask in prayer, you will receive, if you have faith" (Mt 21:21-22).

Similarly, according to St. Mark's report of the fig tree event, when Peter exclaimed, "Rabbi, look! The fig tree that you cursed has withered," Jesus replied, 'Have faith in God. Truly I tell you, if you say to this mountain, 'Be taken up and thrown into the sea,' and if you do not doubt in your heart, but believe that what you say will come to pass, it will be done for you. So I tell you, whatever you ask for in prayer, believe that you have received it, and it will be yours" (Mk 11:20-23). According to this statement, not only did *Jesus* have the power to wither a tree by mere command; *anyone* can have that power and far far more—indeed, anyone can acquire the power to cast a mountain into a sea by mere command!

Another such statement by Jesus can be found in the Gospel according to John, 14:12-14: "Very truly, I tell you, the one who believes in me will also do the works that I do and, in fact, will do greater works than these, because I am going to the Father. I will do whatever you ask in my name, so that the Father may be glorified in the Son. If in my name you ask me for anything, I will do it." Perhaps Jesus meant those statements in a figurative or symbolic sense, but the way they are worded suggests that he meant them literally. Moreover, the story from Matthew and Mark is presented in such a way that it seems clear that we are to believe that Jesus really did wither a fig tree by command.

If Jesus meant these statements literally—"whatever you ask in prayer, you will receive, if you have faith" and "If in my name you ask me for anything, I will do it"—then it seems that his statements were false because millions of people have asked for things in Jesus' name and not received them. If Jesus was wrong, it seems to be a terrible thing to have misled millions of people into thinking that if they want a cure for a terrible disease, or want germ free water, or protection from hurricanes, etc., then all they have to do is ask for it in Jesus' name and have faith that it will occur. They don't have to engage in research or experimentation or preventive actions to solve these problems—and if they do, they are showing a lack of faith! That is, indeed, a hard saying.

3. DIVORCE

Jesus had very strong things to say against divorce. Consider, for example, Matthew 5:31–32: "everyone who divorces his wife, except on the ground of unchastity, makes her an adulteress." That might seem sexist, but Jesus was even handed and also said: "Every [man] who divorces his wife and marries another commits adultery" (Lk 16:18). So if a man divorces his wife and marries another woman, he makes himself an adulterer. Both genders are also covered in Mark's report of Jesus' position: "Whoever divorces his wife and marries another, commits adultery against her; and if she divorces her husband and marries another, she commits adultery" (Mk 10:11–12). These are the scriptural grounds on which the Roman Catholic Church is strictly opposed to divorce (though there are special circumstances under which a marriage can be "annulled").

The preceding quotations are among Jesus' "hard sayings"—hard because Christians are supposed to follow them, but intuitively they don't seem right to many people, including many Catholics. There seem to be plenty of good reasons for divorce in addition to unchastity, which was the only reason that Jesus cited. For example, the following all seem like reasonable grounds for divorce: physical or sexual or emotional abuse of a mate or a child, plus emotional, financial, or sexual abandonment. Most non-Roman Catholic churches accept divorce. Sometimes they justify this acceptance by saying that Jesus did not mean to prohibit divorce in all circumstances; he was trying to protect women in *his* society—a society in which women could not work and earn a living, or live protected, respected lives as single women, so divorce then and there was generally a tragedy for a woman. However, say these critics, times have changed, and if Jesus lived now, he would accept divorce in societies in which women are educated, employable, and protected by law. Other folks think that Jesus was wrong then and would be wrong now to forbid divorce except on the ground of unchastity. (Of course there are also people who think that Jesus meant what he said, meant it without qualification, and was right.)

4. TOLERATING EVIL AND EXTENDING CHARITY

Some of Jesus' other "hard" sayings have to do with how generous and forgiving we should be, and with how we should respond to abusive people. As to the latter, Jesus said that if someone hits us on one side of our face, we should turn our head and offer the other side for the assailant to strike. In Matthew 5:38–42 he says, "Do not resist one who is evil." That suggests that we should, without resistance, allow evil people to steal from us, beat us, rape us, enslave us, torture us, even kill us. This call for nonresistance seems to be because Jesus believed that violent responses to violence only perpetuate an escalating cycle of violence. He wanted us to break that cycle and transform the hearts of evildoers by overcoming evil with love. I'm sure he also believed that if we refrain from responding with violence to evil acts, we will save ourselves from becoming evil, whereas if we fight evil, we, too, will become infected with it. Most Christians, however, believe, or certainly live as though they believe, that Jesus went too far. War and police action are ways of resisting evil, and almost every denomination believes that wars and police actions are sometimes justified. Hence, most Christians believe, in some sense, that Jesus was wrong to tell us in an unqualified way not to resist evil.

Similar things can be said about Jesus' injunction to be charitable. He said, "Give to everyone who begs from you, and do not refuse anyone who wants to borrow from you." That could lead quickly to not having shelter or food for oneself or one's dependents—such as a spouse, children, or elderly parents. Jesus also said we should forgive a person seventy seven times. But if all a person has to do is ask for forgiveness and we are supposed to give it seventy seven times, we will be thoroughly abused and exploited by selfish, cynical, callous, or emotionally disturbed people.

Some Christians believe that Jesus did not mean those injunctions for everyone. They believe that Jesus intended the preceding commands only for his immediate disciples, or only for the few people who are able and willing to follow him perfectly; or they believe he meant his commands with commonsense qualifications that were not stated—such as "Feed the hungry, but don't give away food that your children or feeble parents need."

I hope we all agree with Jesus' belief in the importance of generosity for those who need it, and for forgiving our transgressors when they sincerely ask our forgiveness, rather than being vengeful and unforgiving toward them. I hope we all believe in the possibility and importance of a person's heart being transformed by love. In the twentieth century we saw the power of forgiveness in the lives of Mahatma Gandhi, Martin Luther King Jr., and Nelson Mandela. But I can understand people who believe Jesus went too far in saying, or at least suggesting, that we should not resist evil, should forgive indiscriminately, and should give away our possessions without reservation when asked. (Marcus Borg provides an intriguing possible solution to these purported problems. See his book *Jesus*, chapter 9, section "Nonviolent Resistance," HarperCollins Publishers, 2006.)

5. HATE YOUR PARENTS

Another harsh saying of Jesus is this: "If any one comes to me and does not hate his own father and mother and wife and children and brothers and sisters, yes, and even his own life, he cannot be my disciple" (Lk 14:26–27). Once again, Christians twist and turn trying to explain that Jesus did not mean what is ordinarily meant by such words. Maybe he didn't. Maybe he was compassionately trying to scare away followers because he knew what terrible things lay ahead for them if they followed him. Or maybe he didn't mean "hate" in the sense in which we ordinarily mean it. Perhaps he meant only that his followers must put allegiance to him above allegiance to others. But certainly the ordinary meaning of what he said is troubling.

6. INSENSITIVITY TO ANIMALS

According to Luke 8:26–39, in a region called "Gerasa," Jesus encountered a demented man who was tormented by a legion of demons. The demons begged Jesus not to send them "into the abyss," but, rather, to send them from their human victim into a nearby herd of swine. Jesus granted their request, and then the herd of swine raced down a steep bank into the sea and drowned! Is this a humorous example of "Be careful what you ask for; you might get it"? For it seems the demons were sent into the abyss after all! Nonetheless, what about the poor pigs? Animal lovers may be disturbed by this story. It appears that Jesus used the pigs to destroy the demons when he could have just directly sent the demons "into the abyss" and left the pigs alone.

I hasten to say that we are not told that Jesus himself sent the pigs to their destruction or was indifferent to their demise. Perhaps the entry of the demons into the pigs drove the pigs crazy (but, again, Jesus would be responsible for that), or perhaps the swine were willing agents of Jesus, happily carrying the demons "into the abyss." But there is no indication in the story of sympathy for the pigs. Moreover, there is no reason to think that Jesus was not a meat-eater (although Jews were forbidden to eat the flesh of swine). I can, however, imagine people saying that even though Jesus did not condemn eating meat in his own era (because of nutritional limitations at that time), his love-ethic would lead him to condemn eating meat today, when there is no need for most people to eat meat. Animal lovers might add that if Jesus would not oppose eating meat today, he would not be consistent with his own love-ethic.

7. THE WORLD DID NOT END

In Matthew 24:34 Jesus seems to say clearly that the end of the world would come before the people of his generation all died. (See also Mark 13:30–32 and Luke 21:32–33.) But all those people died, and the world did not come to an end. Hence, it seems that Jesus was mistaken about when the world would end.

8. DANGEROUS RECOMMENDATIONS

In Mark 16:18, Jesus says, "And these signs will accompany those who believe in my name . . . they will pick up serpents, and if they drink any deadly thing, it will not hurt them." Those statements are shocking to many of us. They encourage people to do dangerous, harmful, sometimes deadly things just to demonstrate their faith. Some poisons cannot be survived. Other poisons can be survived, but they inflict serious, permanent damage on a person's throat, stomach, liver, kidneys, or brain. The venom of some snakes, such as the Coral, attacks the nervous system, often inflicting quick, irreversible damage and death. Many New Testament scholars have said that those verses at the end of the Gospel of Mark do not appear to be authentic—and so do not need to be taken seriously. Most Christians, however, do believe they are authentic and that Jesus said those things—yet many of those same people obviously do not believe that what Jesus said is true. If they did, then many more Christians would be picking up venomous serpents and drinking poison in their worship services (as a few Christians still do).

9. BUT THEY DID DIE

In John 6:48–51 Jesus says, "I am the bread of life. Your fathers ate the manna in the wilderness, and they died. This is the bread which comes down from heaven, that a man may eat of it and not die. I am the living bread which came down from heaven; if any one eats of this bread, he will live for ever; and the bread which I shall give for the life of the world is my flesh." In verse 58 he says, "This is the bread which came down from heaven, not such as the fathers ate and died; he who eats this bread will live forever." However, like the fathers of Israel who ate the manna in the wilderness and died, the followers of Jesus "ate his body and drank his blood" yet died. So it seems that Jesus was wrong or misleading when he said that those who ate his flesh would not die as did the fathers of Israel.

CONCLUSION

In my choice and presentation of the preceding reasons for doubting Jesus, I have tried to be "hard hitting" but fair. Yet even if I have been fair, perhaps I haven't been competent; maybe some of the problems that I cited can be explained away by a more adequate understanding of Scripture than I have. However, I do not believe that all of those problems can be explained away. Nonetheless, even if all of the preceding reasons for doubting Jesus are solid, what I want to say now and emphatically is that in my judgment none of those problems, or any others I know of, undermines the overwhelming reasons given in Chapters 1 and 2 for admiring Jesus, loving him, and trying to live the love that he taught and showed us.

Furthermore, I think it is profoundly important that there be churches that embrace people who have any of the above doubts or other doubts about Jesus but who, nonetheless, love him and love the love that he lived and taught. It is therefore important to realize that *Jesus himself* made room for people who doubted him or opposed him or abandoned him, but who loved him. In the next chapter I will provide numerous illustrations of that point.

6

Jesus Accepted Doubters

AT THE BEGINNING OF his public ministry, Jesus called Simon, Andrew, James, and John to leave their jobs as fishermen and follow him. Next he went to Galilee to call Philip to discipleship. Philip accepted Jesus' invitation and was so excited that he hurried to Bethsaida to find his friend Nathanael. To Nathanael he exclaimed, "We have found him about whom Moses in the law and also the prophets wrote, Jesus son of Joseph from Nazareth." Nathanael responded skeptically, "Can anything good come out of Nazareth?" Philip challenged him by replying, "Come and see." Philip did just that, and according to St. John, "When Jesus saw Nathanael coming toward him, he said of him, 'Here is truly an Israelite in whom there is no deceit!'" (John 1:43–47)

What a marvelous example of openness and goodwill on Jesus' part—and Philip's, too! Philip was excited and exclaimed to Nathanael: We have found the Messiah! He is Jesus from Nazareth! Nathanael replied (in so many words), "Get out of here. You've got to be kidding! The Messiah isn't going to come from a little pile of dust like Nazareth!" Philip could have replied, "Suit yourself, you closed-minded bigot," and walked away, but he didn't.

Rather, he reached out to Nathanael again and said: "Come and see." Philip's lack of defensiveness and anger, his persistent openness and positive attitude convinced Nathanael to go with him and take a look at this messiah from nowhere. There is nothing in these verses to suggest that Nathanael followed Philip because his skepticism had weakened. Rather, it seems that Philip was a dear friend, perhaps a close relative, so Nathanael probably followed him out of friendship—not out of conviction or even hope.

When they met Jesus, what was Jesus' reaction to this skeptic from Bethsaida? Did Jesus scorn or reject Nathanael because Nathanael had rejected the idea that Jesus could be the Messiah and had, to make things worse, insulted Jesus' home town? Not at all! Rather, Jesus welcomed him and expressed admiration for Nathanael's intellectual toughness. "Here," said Jesus, "is truly an Israelite in whom there is no deceit!" Here, Jesus was saying, is a candid, intellectually probing person—a person who doesn't accept things on blind faith but, rather, insists on being shown that something is as it is claimed to be! Surely all lovers of Jesus should follow Jesus' lead and Philip's example by welcoming and encouraging those who have doubts about Jesus and by responding respectfully and thoughtfully to their doubts—repeatedly, if necessary.

Another example of Jesus' openness involves Peter. Toward the end of his ministry, when Jesus told his disciples he must undergo great suffering and be killed, Peter rebuked Jesus and told him he must not allow such a thing to happen. Jesus replied to Peter, "Get behind me, Satan! You are a stumbling block to me" Mt 16:21–23. Those are harsh words, but it is understandable that Jesus would say them. By opposing Jesus' final trip to Jerusalem, Peter was saying that Jesus' understanding of his mission in life was wrong-headed and should be abandoned. Consequently, one would think that at that point Jesus would have tossed Peter out on his ear. But Peter wasn't tossed out. He wasn't even shunned. Why? Because Jesus knew that Peter loved him, so Jesus continued to keep him among his closest followers.

Moreover, the preceding misstep by Peter wasn't the last or worst way in which he failed Jesus. After the preceding event, Peter swore to Jesus that he would stick with him through any difficulty or danger, even unto death, but when Jesus was arrested and people tried to connect Peter with Jesus, Peter three times denied even knowing Jesus! Yet Jesus still did not reject Peter! Jesus knew this would happen; when Peter swore his life to Jesus, Jesus predicted to Peter that he would betray him. Jesus knew Peter well and knew he would crumble under the enormous pressure he was about to face, yet Jesus didn't reject Peter then or after his resurrection. Rather, Jesus continued to embrace Peter and gave him a central role in the church.

Another story that illustrates Jesus' acceptance of disciples who opposed him or doubted him is that of the apostle Thomas. The Gospel According to John tells us that three days after Jesus' death and burial, Jesus rose from the dead and appeared to a gathering of his disciples. Thomas was not present at that gathering. He showed up later, but Jesus had left by then. The disciples excitedly told Thomas about Jesus' visit. Thomas, forever after called "Doubting Thomas," found their story wildly implausible and said so. I can just imagine him saying something like, "You guys are crazy. You've had too much wine." Thomas said he did not believe them and would not believe them, "Unless I see the mark of the nails in his hands, and put my finger in the mark of the nails and my hand in his side" (Jn 20:19–29)—which, I think, was Thomas' way of putting an end to the conversation because he didn't think any of that was possible.

Once again, as with Nathanael's skepticism about Jesus, and Peter's opposition to Jesus, we have a situation in which it is natural to expect that when Jesus appeared later to Thomas he criticized him for having so little faith and banished him from among the disciples. But Jesus didn't do that. Rather, he chose to appear again to the disciples when Thomas was present, and he invited Thomas to do exactly what Thomas had said he would need to do in order to believe that Jesus had indeed appeared to the disciples. When Jesus invited Thomas to put his fingers into his wounds, Thomas was convinced.

Once Thomas was convinced that it really was Jesus, Jesus didn't say, "Shame on you, Thomas, oh you of little faith! You should have believed the other disciples! Now go away. I never want to see you again!" Rather, Jesus understood Thomas's doubt, accepted Thomas's doubt, responded to Thomas's doubt, and continued to keep Thomas among his closest followers.

Note also that the other disciples didn't toss Thomas out after he rejected their testimony. There was a full week between the time that Thomas expressed his disbelief and Jesus appeared to him, yet Thomas was still together with the other apostles. Moreover, Nathanael, Thomas, and Peter went on to make important contributions to the church. Surely, therefore, all lovers of Jesus, of whatever denomination, should be accepting of people who admire, love, and want to follow Jesus but who, nonetheless, have serious questions about some of what he said or did.

Conclusion

In John 10:31–33 we are told that certain Jewish leaders who were opposed to Jesus ignored his good deeds and prepared to kill him for blasphemy, that is, for having what they considered to be unorthodox beliefs. Jesus asked them, "For which of my good deeds do you stone me?" Note: Jesus did not say, "For which of my *beliefs* do you stone me?" By focusing attention on his good deeds, rather than his beliefs, Jesus implied that what we should attend to is not what people believe and say doctrinally, but what they *do*. Too often, alas, we follow in the footsteps of Jesus' opponents and we shun or persecute people for what they believe, rather than focusing on how they live. To be sure, love of Jesus requires and encourages study of Scripture and development of thoughtful beliefs, but it doesn't persecute people for the beliefs at which they arrive. Rather, it encourages good deeds and praises them.

In the passage above, Jesus went on to say to his accusers, "If I am not doing the works of my Father, then do not believe me; but if I do them, even though you do not believe me, believe the works, that you may know and understand the Father is in me and I am in the Father" (10:37–38). The importance and centrality of good works, or—more fundamentally—of a loving life, could hardly be emphasized more strongly or elevated more highly than by those words of Jesus in that dangerous situation (remember: he was responding to people who had picked up rocks and were about to stone him to death for what they thought was blasphemy on his part).

We find the same emphasis on works rather than beliefs in Jesus' response to a question from John the Baptist. While John was in prison he sent some of his followers to ask Jesus if he, Jesus, was "the one who is to come," that is, the Messiah. Significantly, Jesus didn't say "yes"; he didn't say, "I am the Son of God"; he didn't tell them what they should believe about him. Rather, he said to John's followers, "Go and tell John what you hear and see: the blind receive their sight, the lame walk, the lepers are cleansed, the deaf hear, the dead are raised, and the poor have good news brought to them" (Mt 11:4–5).

Please note: I am not saying or suggesting that Jesus was promoting salvation by works. Eternal salvation is not something we could ever earn by what we do. Salvation is the free gift of God (Ephesians 2:8–10). The only "work" we need to do is to humbly accept it. But the good work of salvation performed for us by God through Christ is meant to produce people whose lives henceforth issue in good works. Hence, Jesus was saying we should judge whether people, including him, are in a right relationship with God by the works that they do. As Christians we believe it is by the grace of God that we *become* the kinds of people who do the kinds of work that Jesus did and sends us to do. (In Acts 10:34–35 the Apostle Peter is quoted as saying something similar: "I truly understand that God shows no partiality, but in every nation anyone who fears him and does what is right is acceptable to him.")

Part of the significance of the statements by Jesus quoted above is that whereas doctrinal differences may *distinguish* us from one another, they should not *alienate* us from one another. Jesus said, "where two or three are gathered in my name, I am there among them" (Mt 18:20). Awareness of that should have a profound influence on how we Christians relate to one another. We should always be united by our mutual love of Christ, and we should always be united by Christ's love of us. We should always be more strongly united by our mutual love of Christ than we are estranged by our differences. Our fellowship with one another in Christ should be warm, and our service to those in need should be cooperative—whatever our theological or liturgical differences might be.

As a resident of Biloxi, Mississippi, much of which was devastated by Hurricane Katrina on August 29, 2005, I can provide wonderful examples of warm, cooperative service to needy people and animals. Immediately after Hurricane Katrina and right up to the present moment, four years after Katrina, thousands of Christians from a wide range of denominations have poured onto the Mississippi Gulf Coast to provide local residents with free, desperately needed help. These volunteers have helped feed and house thousands of stressed and desolate people; they have helped clean up debris, rebuild homes, provide medical care, and even lift spirits by entertaining us. None of these groups of volunteers limited their help to people from their own denomination. None asked people what they believed before they offered help. All groups just reached out to whomever they could help first. (And such non-discriminatory help was also offered by Jewish, Muslim, Buddhist, secular, and other groups.)

To some people the degree of openness to doubt and to doubters that I am recommending, and my openness to the emergence of new denominations, will seem to have its heart in the right place but be too open theologically; it will not seem specific or demanding enough in terms of what one must believe in order to identify oneself as a Christian or to become a member of a church. As a popular saying goes, "Don't be so open minded that your brain falls out!" But consider again the following facts. Peter frequently misunderstood Jesus; he opposed Jesus at times, and finally even denied that he knew Jesus. But Jesus did not throw Peter out or demote him and elevate someone else above him; nor did the other disciples shun him. Moreover, "Doubting Thomas" told the other disciples, in effect, that they were crazy when they told him that Jesus had risen from the dead and appeared to them. Yet when Jesus later appeared to Thomas, Jesus did not throw Thomas out of his inner circle; he did not even chastise him. Rather, Jesus continued to embrace Thomas, and Peter, because he knew they loved him and were devoted to him. When Jesus decided to return to Bethany to help Lazarus, in spite of the mortal danger in which he was placing himself, it was Thomas who said to the other disciples, "Let us also go, that we may die with him" (Jn 11:16). Now that's love.

Peter showed *his* love in the Garden of Gethsemane. When a mob came to arrest Jesus, Peter drew his sword and stood ready to defend Jesus (Jn 18:10). So yes, Thomas and Peter were imperfect, but Jesus knew they loved him, so he kept them in his embrace. All lovers of Jesus should do the same when we disagree with one another over doctrine, ritual, or interpretation of Scripture. What unites us—Christ's love of us and our love of Christ—should far outshine our differences—like the sun outshines the moon.

It is also important to note that Peter, Thomas, Nathanael, and others, I'm sure, whom Jesus did not reject because of their doubts or disagreements with him, later rose above those doubts or disagreements and became important contributors to the survival and growth of the church. And Saint Paul in his early adulthood was a vigorous persecutor of Christians and the Church! How impoverished the church would have been if Jesus had thrown out all those who ever doubted or opposed him. But, of course, anyone who would have done that, simply would not have been Jesus; he judged people by their hearts—not by their ignorance, doubts, or misguided judgments.

Understandably, theological disagreements sometimes lead to the formation of a new church (as when the Church of England broke off from the Roman Catholic Church, and when the Methodist Church broke off from the Church of England), but none of these differences should render lovers of Jesus hostile to one another. It is the same Lord whom we all love and desire to serve. Jesus did not say that people will know that a person is a Christian by the doctrines that person believes. He did not say, "By this all men will know that you are my disciples: if you believe A, B, and C." Rather, he says in John 13:34–35, "A new commandment I give to you, that you love one another; even as I have loved you, that you also love one another. By this all men will know that you are my disciples, if you have love for one another." What kind of love? The kind that he lived. And we can become that kind of person by devotion to him who was love incarnate and who now comes to us through the Holy Spirit.

Some Christians will disagree with what I am proposing. I hope they will, nonetheless, acknowledge all lovers of Jesus as a part of the Church universal—whether as people who want to affiliate with them but not join, or as people who form a separate group. I hope those who are troubled by my proposal at least tolerate doubters who love Jesus as occupying a way station from which they might one day "graduate" into full membership in their churches. To repeat an earlier point: if a person has a strong conviction that a certain doctrine or ritual or way of organizing is what Christians should believe or do, then that person should find or form an appropriate denomination. But until then and after then our love for Jesus, and Jesus' love for us, should keep alive our love for one another. As Jesus said so magnificently, "A new commandment I give to you, that you love one another; even as I have loved you, that you also love one another. By this all men will know that you are my disciples, if you have love for one another." Amen.

www.ingramcontent.com/pod-product-compliance
Lightning Source LLC
Chambersburg PA
CBHW071438160426
43195CB00013B/1958